BAKE WITH SHIVESH

HarperCollins *Publishers* India

BAKE WITH SHIVESH

HarperCollins *Publishers* India

First published in India by
HarperCollins *Publishers* in 2018
A-75, Sector 57, Noida, Uttar Pradesh 201301, India
www.harpercollins.co.in

2 4 6 8 10 9 7 5 3

P-ISBN: 978-93-5302-311-9
E-ISBN: 978-93-5302-312-6

Designed by HarperCollins *Publishers* India

Printed and bound at
Thomson Press (India) Ltd

To my Nani

CONTENTS

FOREWORD BY POOJA DHINGRA

I still remember the first time I baked brownies. When I was six, my aunt sat me on the kitchen table and made me her assistant. I was mesmerised by the batter and thrilled when I saw the brownies come out of the oven. It was then that I realized – baking is like creating magic. You take simple ingredients like butter, sugar, flour and eggs and transform them into what I like to call 'edible love'. Growing up, baking in India was challenging. Ingredients were difficult to source, ovens were complicated and the most difficult part was finding recipes that work with our climate. Baking has become a lot easier and much more accessible over time, and people like Shivesh have played a big role in being a part of this change.

I met Shivesh years ago. His enthusiasm to become a baker was infectious. Over the years, I've seen him grow into this role. He is sincere, thoughtful, encouraging and tremendously talented. He took to baking easily and makes it look so effortless in his blog and on Instagram.

In 2017, Shivesh worked as an intern at Le15, my cafe and patisserie. During that time, he discovered the sheer hard work involved in running a professional kitchen. In addition to working a shift every day, he also helped me bake and then plate a sit-down dinner for fifty people! He was exceptionally open to doing any task, and receptive to feedback. He hasn't yet been to culinary school but his instincts and abilities have proved that if one is truly self-motivated and disciplined, it is possible to find success.

I really admire the way he uses social media to create a baking community. I've seen him respond to thousands of messages from his followers online, and he is always generous with sharing his knowledge and experiences. Navigating the web and the world of social media may come easy to us millennials, but it isn't the case for most people. This book delves a little deeper into the questions posed online and gives him an opportunity to break down what he has learnt over the years. It will be a valuable addition to the library of anyone working in the food, marketing or photography spaces. His recipes are precise, the styling is always on point and everything on his blog always makes me so hungry!

I love how his writing is relatable;.he makes you want to try baking. You don't need to be a professional chef to make beautiful, simple desserts at home, and who better than Shivesh to get you started?

HDR
PANORAMA
FACE BEAUTY
TAKE PHOTO
VIDEOS

INTRODUCTION

I have always taken my hobbies seriously. As a kid, I was enrolled in all kinds of hobby classes – everything from drawing to abacus. For a brief period, I also took lessons on the Casio. I learnt swimming and dance for the longest time and loved them both. For many years, an art teacher used to come home to teach me painting. In high school, I discovered my love for writing. I won a national level article-writing competition, wrote for a few newspapers, started a blog where I shared my articles and stories and thought I had found my true calling. However, I never sat down to write again after my Class 12 boards, probably because I had found something else I enjoyed more – baking!

I started baking when I was sixteen. The first thing that comes to my mind when I think about baking is my Nani. Every time we went to visit her, besides her warm hug, we were welcomed by the aroma of two freshly baked cakes that were sitting on the counter, waiting to be devoured. She used to always bake a vanilla and a chocolate cake for us. That is my first memory of desserts and also the most special one. In 2013, my Nani suffered a paralytic attack and couldn't enter the kitchen again. On one of our visits to meet her, all the cousins decided to enter the kitchen and bake that chocolate cake that we missed terribly. We rushed to the supermarket and grabbed Betty Crocker pre-mixes and readymade frosting. We decided to make cupcakes and ended up burning an entire batch. I'm almost embarrassed to talk about how those cupcakes looked. Let's not go into how they tasted. But what stayed with me was the fun I had in the kitchen. I used to always sit on the counter while Mum used to bake but I had never thought I'd enjoy doing it myself.

I started baking every other day, whipping up one disaster after another. For the longest time I was making cakes that were best not eaten. But there was something about baking that didn't let me give up on it. I started reading up on baking – the science behind it, the tips and tricks, and kept practising in the kitchen. It took me a lot of time to get better, but I did.

My baking journey would be incomplete without talking about Instagram. When I got onto Instagram, I used to post absolutely anything and everything. It took me a while to discover the 'social' aspect of social media. And when I did, I realized that my baking pictures used to get the best response. I started putting in more time and effort into styling my desserts and photographing them. By this time I had a good number of Instagram followers and thought I was getting better at taking pictures. As an eighteen year old who was taking pictures of his desserts on the terrace and in all other random places, I was thrilled when Instagram picked up one of my pictures and featured it on their feed. I remember my Instagram crashed that evening and I woke up the next day to things that were different and better. Besides a massive bump in the number of followers, I also had media and brands getting in touch. This really encouraged me to keep creating more content and style and photograph my desserts better. The blog happened much later when my Instagram was flooded with requests for recipes. This was all while I was in Hindu College, doing my undergrad in political science.

When I graduated, in June 2017, I decided to pursue blogging full time. While it was an easy decision to take initially, I did question it multiple times over the next six months. All my friends were either applying for post-grad or studying for civil exams. I wasn't sure if I was making the right decision but what I knew was this was what my heart wanted.

I started *Bake with Shivesh* with the idea of sharing my simple recipes with as many with people as I could. I wanted my readers to recreate these recipes in their

own kitchens and not be intimidated by complicated methods and fancy baking terms. I strongly believe that if I can bake, anyone can!

I started out by burning a batch of pre-mix cupcakes and I'm writing a baking book today. It did not call for any professional training, no professional experience and no fancy machines. All I did was to not let failure stop me from entering the kitchen with the excitement to bake something new. All I did was to keep learning and practising.

I've divided the book into four parts – the basics, some wonderful recipes, a styling section followed by a section on photography. I've tried to pack each section with all the knowledge that I've learnt along the way, and hope it helps you bake, style and photograph that perfect dessert.

The fact that simple everyday ingredients like flour, sugar and butter can come together and magically transform into something so beautiful in the oven fascinated me when I first entered the kitchen to bake, and it continues to fascinate me even after five years.

Now let's choose a recipe, enter the kitchen and bake.

BAKING

Let's start with some tips and tricks that'll help make baking a cakewalk.

BEFORE YOU GET STARTED

We can all agree that baking is a supremely satisfying creative process, but that's not all there is to this art. It is also deeply technical and relies heavily on precision. Sometimes, despite our best efforts, the dessert we make may look nothing like the one we wanted, and I'm here to help you avoid this disappointment. Apart from following the steps given in the recipe, here are a few time-tested tips you must keep in mind to ensure that your efforts in the kitchen are always successful.

TIP #1: READ THE RECIPE

Before you start baking, take a moment to go through the recipe properly and understand it. It is always better to have an idea about the instructions before you actually begin work on the dessert. If possible, pre-measure the ingredients and keep them ready. That way, following a recipe in the kitchen will be a breeze and chances of errors will be reduced.

TIP #2: MEASURE YOUR INGREDIENTS RIGHT

It is very important to make sure that all the ingredients the recipe calls for are measured accurately. That's the first step. You must get yourselves a set of measuring cups and measuring spoons. That way you can make sure that you're following the recipe to the T. Always spoon and level the ingredients.

TIP #3: ROOM-TEMPERATURE INGREDIENTS

Unless specified otherwise, please ensure that all your ingredients are at room temperature, especially the butter and eggs. We usually store the butter and eggs in the fridge but when you're baking with them, it becomes crucial to ensure that they're not cold. A recipe that calls for creaming butter and sugar will not work if your butter is cold. It needs to be soft to be able to get to the right consistency and trap air. Room-temperature ingredients incorporate together more easily. If your ingredients are cold, they'll not emulsify as needed and will result in a lumpy batter. However, for desserts like pies or crumbles, you would need cold butter, as specified in the recipe. The cream needs to be cold for it to whip properly. It is also easier to separate eggs when they're cold. When you're making meringue, separate the eggs while they're cold but then let the egg whites come to room temperature before you start beating them – warmer eggs whip faster than cold eggs.

TIP #4: USE THE BEST QUALITY INGREDIENTS

The quality of your ingredients makes a lot of difference to how your dessert turns out. I highly recommend using the best quality ingredients that you can get your hands on. This especially stands true for chocolate and vanilla. Callebaut is the best brand for cooking chocolate. Instead of using vanilla essence, use a pure vanilla extract or vanilla beans. There is nothing like a plump vanilla bean. SPRIG and Goodness Vanilla are good options. I mostly use regular salted Amul Butter for baking. I also use Amul Fresh Cream when I need a light cream for my recipes. If the recipe calls for whipping cream, i.e., cream with 30 per cent fat or more, I use Amul Whipping Cream which is great. Elle & Vire is also an excellent option.

TIP #5: ON FLOUR

I usually use all-purpose flour or maida for baking. It gives the fluffiest and lightest results. Some of the recipes in the book also call for whole-wheat flour, which is a healthier substitute for all-purpose flour. You can always replace whole wheat with all purpose in my recipes but vice-versa does not always work. A couple of recipes in the book also call for buckwheat flour or kuttu ka aata. Buckwheat is not related to wheat at all and is naturally gluten free. It has a strong, nutty taste and cannot be used as a substitute for all-purpose flour. Another gluten-free flour used in this book is polenta flour that is made by grinding corn. This flour has a rich yellow colour and gives a nice grainy texture to the dessert. It is different from cornflour that I use to thicken fruit fillings or in cookies to make them chewy. To make oat flour, simply pulse traditional/ rolled oats in a food processor until they're ground into a powder like consistency. This only takes a minute or lesser. Similarly, to make almond flour or almond meal, process whole almonds (I don't blanch them) in the food processor and sieve it once. Make sure you don't process them for too long otherwise you'll be left with almond butter.

TIP #6: ON SUGAR

Most of my recipes call for castor sugar (also known as superfine or breakfast sugar). I avoid using granulated sugar for baking. The particles of granulated sugar are too big and don't always melt in the oven completely. I use granulated sugar only when I'm heating it on the stove. I also don't use powdered sugar in baking (unless the recipe calls for it) because it doesn't give the structure that castor sugar does. I use powdered sugar when I'm making frosting. I always recommend sifting icing sugar before using it because it tends to have lumps. Trust is a good brand for castor sugar. I use Mawana icing sugar. I also use lightly packed brown sugar (also known as soft brown sugar) in a lot of my recipes. Tate + Lyle is the best brand available in the Indian market for that. If the recipe calls for brown sugar, please don't substitute it with white sugar. Although it would not alter your dessert completely, brown sugar makes the dessert moister because of its higher molasses content. I usually use soft brown sugar for my cookie recipes because I like them to be soft and chewy. Using only white sugar will make a very crisp cookie.

TIP #7: ON CHOOSING FRUITS AND BERRIES

I love baking with fresh fruits and berries. Always pick fresh fruits and berries over dried or canned ones. I would use dried fruits and berries only in granolas, cookies, biscotti or in recipes where fresh ones wouldn't work. Fresh berries are expensive and not always available but please don't substitute fresh berries with frozen ones. If you're in Delhi, you can source fresh berries from INA Market/ Khan Market/ Foodhall/ Modern Bazaar. I use frozen berries for compotes and fillings. If you can't get berries, you can substitute them with other tart fruits.

TIP #8: CHECK THE EXPIRY DATE

If you don't bake too often, it is very important to check the expiry date of ingredients before you get baking. This is especially important for levelling agents like baking soda and baking powder. I make sure I buy a new sachet or small box of fresh yeast every time I want to use it. If your yeast has expired, it'll not be able to do its job.

TOOLS OF THE TRADE

Besides the very essential set of measuring cups or a weighing scale, there are some tools you must get if you want to bake regularly and properly.

1. You don't need to invest into a stand mixer but if you can, get an electric mixer. An electric mixer makes life very easy when you need to whip the cream or make meringue.
2. A basic whisk is a kitchen essential. Use it to incorporate air into your batter. My favourite baking tool is a rubber spatula with a wooden handle. It comes handy when I want to fold the dry ingredients into wet ingredients. Since it is also heat resistant, it comes handy when I'm making caramel or fillings on the stove. It also helps be get every drop of the batter out of the mixing bowl into the pan.
3. Besides that, an offset spatula is a great tool to have – I use it to frost the cakes.
4. It is very important to have a few large mixing bowls. Try and keep at least one stainless steel bowl.
5. You would also need a mini grater or a zester.

6. Always stock up on plastic wrap and parchment paper.

TIP #1 INVEST IN THE RIGHT BAKEWARE

If you love baking, bakeware is something you must invest in. You'll be surprised to see how much difference the bakeware makes. I usually use metal bakeware. Metal is a great conductor of heat. They heat quickly and also cool quickly too once out of the oven. Aluminium bakeware is a great option and I like to stay away from silicon moulds (silicon mats are great, though!). While it's easier to get the cake out of a silicon mould, nothing comes close to the crisp dark crust that metal bakeware achieves.

Glass is also a poor conductor of heat. I only use glass bakeware for fruit crisps and crumbles. Glass retains the heat even once it's out of the oven and keeps the dessert warm. So, something like a cobbler or a pudding that needs to be served warm can be made in glass bakeware. Ceramic bakeware is also not a very popular choice but definitely looks pretty on the table. If a dessert needs to be served in the dish or eaten out of the dish, ceramic is ideal. I love using ceramic pie dishes and ramekins. But for heavy baking, stick to metal bakeware.

TIP #2 PREP YOUR PAN

You win half the battle by getting your hands on the right bakeware. What follows is prepping it right. It is heart-breaking to have your cake stuck to the pan and then breaking it when attempting to pull it out. It's better to grease it properly than to go through all the trouble. I always generously brush my pans with melted/softened butter before pouring the batter into it.

When it comes to prepping, make parchment paper your best friend. Lining your pans with parchment will ensure your cake always comes out smoothly. If you don't have parchment paper, brush your pan with melted butter and dust it with flour. Don't forget to tap out the excess flour. Use cocoa powder if you're making a chocolate cake. If you've dusted your pans with flour and cocoa, let the pans sit in the freezer while you get the batter ready.

TIP #3 UNDERSTAND YOUR OVEN

Every oven works differently and to make sure you get your baked good right each time, it's very important to understand your oven. If you usually end up burning what you're baking, your oven is probably hotter – you should bake at a lower temperature than what is mentioned in the recipe and check on the cake a little earlier than the mentioned time. If you are using a convection oven, you need to reduce the temperature slightly from the ones stated in the recipes.

TIP #4 KEEP YOUR OVEN DOOR CLOSED

It is very tempting to keep opening the oven door to check on the progress of your dessert. But doing this is not a good idea. Every time you open your oven door, all the hot air rushes out, which messes up with the temperature. This can result in your cakes deflating. For an unobstructed baking process, keep your oven door closed. Open it only if you want to rotate your baking tray or closer to the baking time mentioned in the recipe to see if the cake is done.

TIP #5 REST AND CHILL, WHEN REQUIRED

A lot of recipes call for resting the dough in the fridge. It can be tempting to skip the resting part and skip to the next step. However, it's a crucial step that you must not avoid. When you're making a tart crust or a pie crust, chilling the dough could be required to make it firm enough to be rolled out. Once I line my tart pans with the dough, I always let them sit the fridge so that they don't shrink in the oven. I also always chill my cookie dough before I pop them into the oven. That helps solidify the butter in the dough and lets the liquid be absorbed in the dough properly. The solid butter doesn't melt as quickly in the oven and ensures that the cookies don't spread too much. However, you must not let your cake batter sit around for too long.

TIP #6 BE PATIENT

Baking calls for a lot of patience. Make sure you have time on your hands before you dive into it. You don't want to rush through the process. Once your cakes/cupcakes are out of the oven, let them cool completely before you try to pull them out of the pan. Hot cakes are very delicate and are more likely to fall apart. You must also make sure that your cakes are completely cooled before you begin to frost them. The frosting will melt if the cake is still warm. Once the cookies are out of the oven, I recommend letting them rest on the baking tray for at least 10 minutes before you lift them off. Chances of them breaking are higher when they're fresh out of the oven. Desserts like cheesecakes and panna cottas take a lot of time to set. It is important to be patient and give them the time they need.

GET YOUR BASICS RIGHT

METHODS

HOW TO CREAM

Most recipes start with 'creaming' the fat with sugar. This is a crucial step and helps make sure that your cake is light and airy. Don't hasten through this step. In creaming, you incorporate air into the batter. I usually give it a good 5 minutes when using an electric mixer on high speed. If you're using a hand whisk, it'll take longer. Go for the fluffy!

HOW TO CUT IN

Cutting in is a process of combining fat and flour to achieve a flaky and tender texture. Pie crust and tart recipes call for this process. You can either use a pastry blender, a food processor or just your hands. When you're cutting in the butter, make sure it is cold – you want to preserve shards of butter in the mixture, which is what gives the pastry its flaky texture. I pulse using a food processor until the texture is sandy with small chunks of butter.

HOW TO FOLD

Getting this step right completely changed baking for me. When I started baking, most of my cakes would turn out dense. I started reading up to find out where I was going wrong and as it turned out, I was committing the baking sin of overmixing my batter. When you combine your wet and dry ingredients, it is very important to not overmix or mix too vigorously. I ditch the electric mixer when I reach this step and grab a spatula. The idea is to gently fold in the dry ingredients into the wet ingredients until you see no flour pockets. If you overbeat the batter, you'll knock out all the air that you incorporated during creaming. The result will be a dense cake! You've to also be very gentle when you're folding in ingredients into whipped cream or whipped egg whites. Do the folding right and say bye-bye to dense cakes forever.

HOW TO ROLL OUT

When you're making tarts, pies or galettes, you'll need to roll out the dough. Before you do this, make sure that your dough is well rested and at the right temperature. If the dough is too soft, it'll stick and break. You'll be unable to roll it out if it's too cold. The idea is to let the dough rest in the fridge until it firms up and then allow it to thaw for 5 minutes on the kitchen counter before rolling it out. To roll out the dough, dust the kitchen counter with flour or icing sugar. This will prevent it from sticking. Be sure to also lightly dust the rolling pin. The other option is to roll out the dough by keeping it between two sheets of parchment paper.

While rolling out, if the dough begins to break, you can simply start over. If the dough becomes too soft, pop it back into the fridge to firm up.

HOW TO MAKE WHIPPED CREAM

A lot of recipes of the book call for whipped cream. It simply means a cream with 30 per cent + fat that has not been beaten. Heavy cream is cream with fat content of over 36 per cent. You cannot whip a cream that has a fat content of less than 30 per cent.
To make whipped cream, make sure the whipping cream is cold. Don't take it out of the fridge until you're ready to whip. On hot summer days, I also let the mixing bowl and mixer blades sit in the freezer for a while. You can use a stand mixer or an electric mixer to whip the cream. You can also whip it by hand using a whisk but that will take time. Using an ice-bath will help. Always use a metal bowl.

If the recipe calls for 'cream whipped to soft peaks', beat for 5-6 minutes or until you start seeing trails in the cream. For firm or stiff peaks, continue beating the cream for over 10 minutes – the cream will become more voluminous, stiffer and its peaks will have a firm structure. Do not change the speed and direction of your mixer.

HOW TO BEAT EGG WHITES INTO MERINGUE

To beat egg whites into meringue, make sure your eggs are separated properly and there are no traces of egg yolks in your whites. Also, ensure that the bowl and beaters are clean and grease-free. There should be no water droplets in the bowl. Use a metal or a glass bowl for whipping up the egg whites. Do not use plastic bowls here. Whipping up egg whites using a hand whisk is a time-consuming and tiring task, so try and use a hand mixer or an electric mixer for this.

Begin by beating the egg whites on high speed. The egg whites will become frothy. This is when you start adding sugar – little quantities at a time while the mixer is still running. The egg whites will begin to gain volume and form soft peaks. Keep mixing until the egg whites become glossy and the peaks become stiff. The test is to see if the meringue is done to turn the bowl upside down. If nothing falls off, your meringue is done. Or rub a little meringue between your fingers – if you don't feel any sugar particles, you're good to go.

HOW TO MELT CHOCOLATE

Melting chocolate can be tricky and you need to be very careful while doing this. If you overdo it, even if by just a little, your chocolate will burn and there is no recovery from that.

You can melt your chocolate in the microwave in 30-second bursts. Heat it in the microwave for 30 seconds, then take it out and give it a stir. Do this till most of the chocolate is melted. If you can see only a few chunks, just keep mixing it by hand until the chunks melt from latent heat.

The other option is to melt the chocolate on a double boiler. Do not attempt to melt chocolate in a container set over direct flame. The chances of burning increase. Melted chocolate should be smooth and lump free. It becomes thick and lumpy if you overheat it. Make sure that the chocolate does not come in contact with water. The bowl that you're using to melt the chocolate should be completely dry. Even a small quantity of water can make the chocolate seize.

HOW TO MAKE A DOUBLE BOILER

To make a double boiler, fill 1/4th of a saucepan with water and set it over medium heat. Let the water come to a simmer. Then, place another bowl or saucepan over it. The steam from the bottom saucepan rises and heats the bowl on the top. This indirect heat allows the contents of the bowl to heat slowly. Make sure that the water in the saucepan does not touch the bowl on the top.

HOW TO MAKE AN ICE BATH

To make an ice bath, fill a large bowl with ice and water. Place the other bowl on this ice to quickly cool down its contents. I use an ice bath to whip cream during the summer or to cool down a filling or sauce quickly, but evenly. Make sure the water from the ice bath does not enter the other bowl.

HOW TO MAKE A WATER BATH

To make a water bath, place the baking pan in a larger oven-safe dish. Add about an inch of hot water to the larger dish so that it surrounds the baking pan. I use a water bath when I'm baking a cheesecake or a custard pie. Using a water bath adds moisture in the oven. It provides slower and more even heating, the kind that prevents a cheesecake or custard filling from cracking.

CONVERSION TABLE

PRODUCT	1 CUP	1/2 CUP	1/4 CUP
FLOUR	120G	60G	30G
BUTTER	220G	110G	55G
CASTOR SUGAR	220G	110G	55G
BROWN SUGAR	200G	100G	50G
ICING SUGAR	120G	60G	30G
LIQUID	200G	100G	50G

1 Tablespoon: 15g

1 Teaspoon: 5g

RECIPES

Now that you have the basics up your sleeve, let's get those hands dirty and start baking.

EGGLESS

WHOLE-WHEAT PLUM GALETTE

Juicy plums with a kick of orange zest and cinnamon, nestled into a flaky whole-wheat pastry, topped with a large scoop of ice cream, is all that you need sometimes.

FOR CRUST

1 cup whole-wheat flour
¼ cup rolled oats
½ cup cold butter, cubed
4 tablespoons granulated sugar
4 tablespoons ice-cold water

FOR FILLING

¼ cup ground almonds
8-10 plums, thinly sliced
¼ cup lightly packed brown sugar
½ teaspoon cinnamon powder
1 tablespoon orange zest
1 egg + splash of milk to brush

PROCEDURE

1. In a food processor, combine whole-wheat flour, oats, cold butter and sugar.
2. The mixture will have a sandy texture. Add in the cold water and pulse until the mixture begins to hold together when pinched.
3. Flatten the dough into a disk. Wrap it in plastic wrap and refrigerate for 30 minutes.
4. Meanwhile, make the filling. Combine the plums, brown sugar and orange zest.
5. Preheat the oven to 200°C.
6. On a parchment, roll out the dough into a circle of about ¼-inch thickness.
7. Leaving 1-inch borders around the edge, evenly spread the ground almonds on the rolled-out dough.
8. Arrange the plum slices on the layer of ground almonds.
9. Fold the edges of the galette over the fruit.
10. Generously brush the overlapped edges with egg wash (egg lightly beaten with a splash of milk). Simply brush with milk if you want to avoid using egg.
11. Bake at 200°C for 20-30 minutes or until the crust is golden-brown.
12. Let it cool on the baking tray completely before lifting. Serve with whipped cream or vanilla ice cream.

ORANGE CHIFFON CAKE

Chiffon cakes have always fascinated me. They're like edible flavoured clouds that you can easily bake in your kitchen. How dreamy is that!

CAKE

7 eggs, separated

1½ cups castor sugar, separated

2 cups all-purpose flour

2 teaspoons baking powder

1 teaspoon baking soda

½ teaspoon salt

1 tablespoon orange zest

¾ cup fresh orange juice

½ cup vegetable oil

COMPOTE

2 cups fresh gooseberries, removed from their husks

½ cup granulated sugar

¼ cup water

1 teaspoon orange zest

PROCEDURE

1. Preheat the oven to 170°C and generously brush an 8-inch Bundt pan with melted butter.

2. Using an electric mixer, beat the egg whites on high speed until they become foamy. While the mixer is still running, gradually add ½ cup castor sugar. Keep beating until the egg whites form stiff peaks.

3. In a separate bowl, combine 1 cup castor sugar, flour, baking powder, baking soda, salt and orange zest together.

4. Make a well and add egg yolks, orange juice and vegetable oil to the dry ingredients. Using a spatula, gently mix it together until everything is well combined.

5. Very gently, fold the whipped egg whites into the batter in batches. Be careful to not mix vigorously and knock out the air.

6. Transfer the batter into the prepared cake pan and bake it at 170°C for 40-50 minutes or until a skewer inserted into the centre comes out clean.

7. To make the cape gooseberry compote, combine all the ingredients in a saucepan and cook them on medium heat.

8. Cook until the gooseberries begin to break down and the compote becomes thick. Take it off the heat and let it cool completely.

EGGLESS

FROZEN MANGO CHEESECAKE

Imagine bringing out this elegant dessert on a summer brunch table – a crunchy layer of macadamia crust and a no-bake layer of cream cheese with mango puree, topped with fresh fruit. Total winner!

BASE

½ cup ground macadamia nuts
½ cup all-purpose flour
½ cup castor sugar
½ cup softened butter

CHEESECAKE

1 cup heavy cream
¼ cup castor sugar
1 cup cream cheese, softened
1 cup mango puree

Fresh fruit to top

PROCEDURE

1. Preheat the oven to 180°C.
2. In a large bowl, combine all the ingredients for the cheesecake base. It will be a soft, doughy consistency..
3. Use your fingers to evenly spread a layer of this dough in a 15-cm ring placed on a baking tray lined with a silicon mat.
4. Bake the base at 180°C for 20 minutes or until it is golden-brown. Let it cool completely.
5. To make the filling, beat all the ingredients together until the mixture is smooth and lump free.
6. Pour the filling on the cooled crust. Let it rest in the freezer for 4-5 hours or overnight.
7. Before serving, top with fresh fruit and serve while it is still cold.

EGGLESS

STRAWBERRY FIG PIE

If making pies intimidates you, shed all your inhibitions, get into the kitchen and make this one with me. The only way to bake a pie is to bake a pie.

PIE CRUST

1¼ cup whole-wheat flour
2 tablespoons granulated sugar
⅓ cup unsalted butter, cold and cubed
1-2 tablespoons cold water
Egg wash (**1** egg, lightly beaten with a splash of milk. If you want to avoid eggs, simply use milk to brush the pie dough.)
2 tablespoons castor sugar, to top the unbaked pie

FILLING

2 cups fresh/frozen strawberries, sliced
½ cup figs, sliced
½ cup castor sugar
¼ teaspoon cardamom powder
2 tablespoons lemon juice
2 tablespoons cornflour

PROCEDURE

1. In a food processor, mix flour, sugar and butter until it resembles a coarse meal. Add water and mix until the dough comes together.
2. Divide the dough into two halves and wrap them in plastic wrap separately. Let the dough chill in the refrigerator for at least 1 hour before you begin rolling it out.
3. To make the filling, combine strawberries, figs, sugar, cardamom powder, lemon juice and cornflour in a large bowl.
4. Preheat the oven to 180°C.
5. Dust a clean surface lightly with flour. Roll out one half of the dough into a ⅛-inch thick circle. Press it into the bottom and sides of a pie dish. Trim the pie dough along the edge of the dish. If the dough feels too soft, let it rest in the refrigerator for longer. If the pie dough cracks while working, roll it out again or simply use a wet finger to fix the crack.
6. Transfer the strawberry-fig filling into the pie dish.
7. Roll out the other half of the dough into a ⅛-inch circle. Use cookie cutters to cut out flowers and leaves from the dough. Carefully lift and place these along the edges of the pie dish.
8. Brush the pie with egg wash and sprinkle with the castor sugar.
9. Bake the pie at 180°C for 40-45 minutes until the pie crust is golden-brown.

LEMON-CREAM CAKE

This three-layer lemon-cream cake is just how I imagine my 'when life gives you lemons' life.

INGREDIENTS

1 cup unsalted butter, softened
2½ cups all-purpose flour
4 teaspoons baking powder
1 teaspoon salt
1½ tablespoons lemon zest
1 cup castor sugar
2 whole eggs
3 egg yolks
4 tablespoons fresh lemon juice
¾ cup milk

FOR FILLING

½ cup lemon curd
2 cups sweetened whipped cream

FOR CURD

4 eggs
½ cup granulated sugar
4 tablespoons fresh lemon juice
4 tablespoons unsalted butter
1 tablespoon lemon zest

PROCEDURE

1. Preheat the oven to 180°C. Line three 8-inch cake pans with parchment paper.
2. In a bowl, whisk together flour, baking powder, salt and lemon zest.
3. In a separate bowl, cream together butter and sugar until the mixture becomes light and fluffy.
4. Add eggs and egg yolks one at a time. Beat properly after each addition. Beat in the lemon juice.
5. Alternately add the flour mixture and milk into the wet ingredients. Do not over-mix but make sure there are no flour pockets.
6. Divide the batter equally and pour into the cake tins. Bake for about 20-30 minutes or until a toothpick inserted into the centre comes out clean.
7. Once the cakes have cooled completely, fill and layer them generously with lemon curd and whipped cream.

LEMON CURD

1. In a saucepan, combine eggs, sugar and fresh lemon juice. Set it over medium heat and stir continuously. Keep stirring to prevent the eggs from curdling.
2. Cook until the mixture is thick enough to coat the back of a spoon. Now take it off the heat and sieve it into a clean, large bowl.
3. Immediately add butter and lemon zest and mix till everything is well combined.
4. Cover with a plastic wrap touching the surface of the curd. Let it cool completely.

EGGLESS

CHURRO COOKIES

In 2016, on my Christmas trip to London, I had these unforgettable, incredible churros at Winter Wonderland. These cinnamon sugar churro cookies dunked in chocolate remind me of that warm, fuzzy feeling.

INGREDIENTS

2 cups water
6 tablespoons granulated white sugar
4 tablespoons vegetable oil
2 cups all-purpose flour
Vegetable oil, for frying
1 cup castor sugar + **2 tablespoons** cinnamon powder
A pinch of salt

PROCEDURE

1. In a saucepan set over medium heat, combine water, granulated white sugar, vegetable oil and salt. Bring the mixture to a boil and remove from heat.
2. While the mixture is still hot, immediately add the flour and mix well until the dough thickens and there are no lumps of flour. Let the dough cool at room temperature.
3. Transfer the dough to a piping bag attached to a large star tip.
4. On a baking tray lined with parchment paper, pipe the churro dough into circles, starting from the centre and then piping around it.
5. Let the baking tray sit in the freezer for 20-30 minutes or until the churro cookies are firm.
6. Heat the oil for frying. Lift the churro cookies off the baking tray and gently drop them in the hot oil for frying.
7. Once the cookies are golden-brown on both sides, transfer them to a plate lined with paper towels. Get rid of the excess oil, then dunk them into the castor sugar and cinnamon mixture.
8. Dip the churro cookies into melted chocolate and eat while they're still hot.

GRAPEFRUIT TIRAMISU

I don't usually mess around with classics but when I do I make sure they're equally impressive.

INGREDIENTS

1 cup mascarpone cheese, at room temperature
½ teaspoon cardamom powder
1 tablespoon grapefruit zest, freshly grated
1 cup whipping cream
½ cup castor sugar
⅓ cup grapefruit juice, freshly squeezed
¼ cup water
⅓ cup granulated sugar
9-10 ladyfinger biscuits
Cocoa powder, for dusting

SERVING SUGGESTION

You can make orange tiramisu by replacing grapefruit juice and grapefruit zest with orange juice and orange zest..

PROCEDURE

1. Combine the mascarpone cheese, cardamom powder and grapefruit zest.
2. Using an electric mixer, beat the whipping cream until soft peaks form.
3. Keep beating and add 1 tablespoon of castor sugar at a time. Continue beating the cream until stiff peaks form.
4. Gently fold the mascarpone cheese into the whipped cream and let it sit in the refrigerator.
5. Meanwhile, bring the grapefruit juice, water and sugar to a boil.
6. Cook until the sugar melts completely. Transfer the syrup to a shallow dish.
7. Break the ladyfinger biscuits into half and dip them into the grapefruit juice syrup. Place them in dessert glasses.
8. Pipe the mascarpone–cardamom cream on top of the ladyfinger biscuits. Dust generously with cocoa powder.
9. Repeat these layers once again.
10. Let the tiramisu glasses chill in the refrigerator for at least 30 minutes before serving.

SESAME GOLDEN MATCHA PIE

This is a slightly elaborate recipe that you should take up for a day when you're feeling experimental and want to bake something stunning with very interesting flavours.

SESAME PIE CRUST

1 cup all-purpose flour
¼ cup black sesame seeds, lightly toasted
2 tablespoons granulated sugar
⅓ cup unsalted butter, cold and cubed
1-2 tablespoons cold water

MATCHA CUSTARD

1 cup castor sugar
2 tablespoons all-purpose flour
4 teaspoons golden matcha powder
½ cup butter, melted
4 eggs
2 cups heavy cream

SERVING SUGGESTION

Let the pie rest in the fridge for at least 3 hours before serving.

PROCEDURE

1. Preheat the oven to 180°C.
2. In a food processor, mix flour, sugar, sesame seeds and butter until it resembles a coarse meal. Add water and mix until the dough comes together.
3. Flatten the dough and wrap it in plastic wrap. Let the dough chill in the refrigerator for at least 1 hour before you begin rolling it out.
4. Reserve ¼ of the dough to make the design on the top of the custard filling. On a lightly floured surface, roll out rest of the dough into a ⅛-inch circle. Carefully transfer it into the bottom and up the edges of an 8-inch pie dish. Trim the edges.
5. Place a sheet of parchment paper on the pie shell and fill it with pie weights/ pulses. Bake at 180°C for 15-20 minutes.
6. To make the golden matcha custard, combine the sugar, flour and golden matcha powder together.
7. Whisk in the melted butter.
8. Add eggs, one at a time, and beat well after each addition. Beat in the heavy cream.
9. Strain the filling and pour it into the half-baked pie crust.
10. To make the design on top, roll out the leftover dough into a ⅛-inch thick circle. Use a knife to carve out the design of your choice. Place it on top of the custard.

11. Bake the pie at 180°C for 40-50 minutes or until the custard around the edges starts to set but is still wobbly in the centre. The custard will continue to cook as it cools down.

12. Once baked, let the pie cool at room temperature.

STRAWBERRY SESAME CAKE

I'm not sure which aspect of this recipe I like more – the unusual combination of flavours or the fact that you can simply throw everything into the food processor to make this cake.

INGREDIENTS

1 cup milk + **1 teaspoon** white vinegar
2½ cups all-purpose flour
½ cup finely ground black sesame seeds
2 teaspoons baking powder
1 teaspoon baking soda
3 eggs
1 teaspoon lemon zest
⅓ cup castor sugar
¼ cup vegetable oil
10-12 strawberries, sliced

PROCEDURE

1. Preheat the oven to 180°C. Line an 11x4-inch loaf pan with parchment paper.
2. Add white vinegar to milk. Mix and let it rest for 5 minutes.
3. In a large food-processor bowl, add milk, flour, ground sesame seeds, baking powder, baking soda, eggs, lemon zest, sugar and vegetable oil.
4. Process until everything is well combined and the batter is ready. There should be no flour pockets.
5. Transfer the batter into the lined loaf pan and top it with sliced strawberries.
6. Bake at 180°C for 30-40 minutes until a skewer inserted into the loaf comes out clean.

EGGLESS, GLUTEN FREE

BUCKWHEAT CARAMEL TART

This eggless, gluten-free dessert is an absolute delight. With the luscious caramel filling and nuts in a buckwheat crust, it is comfort baked in a tart pan.

BASE

1 tablespoon ground flaxseeds

2 + ½ **tablespoons** water

½ **cup** butter, softened

1 teaspoon cinnamon powder

⅓ **cup** soft brown sugar

1 + ¼ **cup** buckwheat flour

¼ **cup** almond flour

FILLING

1 cup soft brown sugar

1 cup butter

½ **teaspoon** vanilla extract

¼ **cup** heavy cream

1 + ½ **cup** assorted nuts

PROCEDURE

1. Combine ground flaxseeds and water. Mix well and let it rest for 5 minutes.

2. Start by beating butter and cinnamon with sugar. Beat in the flaxseed mixture.

3. Fold in the buckwheat flour and almond flour. Mix until the dough comes together.

4. Press the dough into the bottom and up the sides of a 14x4.5-inch rectangular tart pan. Refrigerate for 30 minutes.

5. Preheat the oven to 200°C. Once the tart is chilled, prick it using a fork.

6. Bake for 10-15 minutes. Remove from the oven and reduce the temperature to 180°C.

7. To make the filling, cook sugar, cream, butter and vanilla in a saucepan set over medium heat. Bring it to a boil. Set if off heat and mix in the assorted nuts.

8. Transfer the filling into the tart shell. Bake at 180°C for 20-25 minutes.

9. Once baked let the tart set in the fridge for 15-20 minutes.

EGGLESS

RASPBERRY MOUSSE

I wish all simple desserts looked so elegant. This mousse is my go-to pick when something quick, appealing and pleasurable has to be served.

RASPBERRY MOUSSE

1 cup frozen raspberries

¼ cup granulated sugar

4 tablespoons lemon juice

1 tablespoon cornflour

1 tablespoons water

1 cup whipping cream

CRUMBLE

¾ cup traditional oats

½ cup whole-wheat flour

4 tablespoons honey

¼ cup cold butter, cubed

PROCEDURE

1. In a saucepan set over medium heat, cook frozen raspberries, sugar and lemon juice until the sugar melts and the raspberries begin to break down.

2. In a small bowl, combine cornflour and water. Add the slurry to the saucepan in which the raspberries are cooking.

3. After adding the cornflour, bring the mixture to a boil. Then set it off heat and let it cool completely.

4. Meanwhile, using an electric mixer, beat the whipping cream until it forms stiff peaks.

5. Carefully fold in the cooled raspberry mixture into the whipped cream. Do not over-beat otherwise the whipped cream will deflate.

6. Refrigerate the mousse and make the honey-oat crumble.

7. To make the crumble, preheat the oven to 200°C.

8. In a large bowl, combine oats, wheat flour and honey.

9. Using your fingers, combine the cold butter into the oat-flour mixture until it reaches a coarse-sandy texture.

10. Spread the crumble on baking tray lined with a silicon mat or a parchment paper. Bake for 10-15 minutes or until it becomes golden-brown.

11. To assemble the mousse, add a generous layer of crumble to a glass. Pipe the mousse on top of the crumble and top with fresh/frozen raspberries.

ETON MESS CAKE

The strawberry plants I grew at home while working on this book inspired me to bake this two-layer cake filled with fluffy whipped cream, fresh strawberries and crushed meringue kisses. Gorgeous, isn't it?

CAKE

4 cups all-purpose flour
4 teaspoons baking powder
2 cups castor sugar
1 cup vegetable oil
4 eggs or **2 cups** Greek yogurt
1 teaspoon pure vanilla extract
1 cup milk

FROSTING

2 cups whipping cream
½ cup icing sugar

MERINGUE KISSES

4 egg whites
2 cups castor sugar

TOPPINGS

Fresh strawberries
Edible flowers
Maple syrup, to drizzle

PROCEDURE

1. To make the cake, preheat the oven to 180°C. Line two 8-inch cake pans with parchment paper.
2. In a bowl, whisk flour and baking powder together.
3. In a separate bowl, beat the vegetable oil and sugar until the mixture is light and pale.
4. Beat in the eggs one at a time and beat well after each addition. If you're using Greek yogurt instead of eggs, this is when you add it to the mixture.
5. Mix in the vanilla extract.
6. Fold the dry ingredients into the wet ingredients in three batches, alternating with milk.
7. Pour the batter into the prepared cake pans and bake at 180°C for 30-40 minutes. Once baked, let the cakes cool completely.
8. To make the meringue kisses, preheat the oven to 100°C.
9. Beat the egg whites using an electric mixer on high speed until soft peaks form.
10. While the mixer is still running, start adding sugar, one tablespoon at a time.
11. Beat until the egg whites form stiff peaks. Transfer the meringue into a piping bag attached to a round tip.
12. On a baking tray lined with parchment paper, pipe the meringue in the shape of kisses. Bake these at 100°C for an hour and store in airtight container.
13. Using an electric mixer, beat the whipping cream and sugar until soft peaks form.

14. To assemble the cake, cover one layer with whipped cream, crushed meringue kisses and fresh strawberries.

15. Place the other layer on the top. Generously cover the cake with whipped cream, strawberries, meringue kisses and edible flowers. Drizzle with maple syrup.

EGGLESS

BANANA CHOCOLATE LOAF CAKE

I've only recently discovered my love for chocolate and banana together and it doesn't get better than this eggless loaf cake. You can also make it in a round cake pan. Be sure to use Greek yogurt and not the curd we make at home.

INGREDIENTS

1½ cups all-purpose flour

¾ cup cocoa powder

½ teaspoon baking soda

1 teaspoon baking powder

4 bananas + **1** for top

¾ cup vegetable oil

1 cup castor sugar

4 tablespoons Greek yogurt

Handful of cocoa nibs

PROCEDURE

1. Line a loaf pan with parchment paper.
2. Combine all-purpose flour, cocoa powder, baking soda and baking powder in a bowl.
3. In an oven preheated to 200°C, bake 4 whole bananas, with their skin on for 5 minutes. Their skin will turn black and the bananas will become mushy.
4. Preheat the oven to 180°C.
5. Once the bananas have cooled down, mash them in a large bowl.
6. Add vegetable oil, castor sugar and yogurt. Beat well.
7. Using a spatula, fold the dry ingredients into the wet, making sure there are no flour pockets in the batter.
8. Transfer the batter into the prepared loaf pan. Placed a sliced banana on the top. Sprinkle cocoa nibs.
9. Bake the cake at 180°C for 30-40 minutes or until a toothpick inserted into the centre comes out clean.

NO-BAKE MANGO PIE

This no-bake mango pie with a kick of lime is a blessing on hot summer days when I crave for a mango dessert but something that doesn't require me to heat up the oven.

INGREDIENTS

2½ cups digestive biscuits, crushed
1¼ cups butter, melted
½ cup coconut milk (or water)
1 tablespoon gelatine powder
2 cups mango pulp
180 grams cream cheese, softened
¼ teaspoon lime zest
¼ cup castor sugar

SERVING SUGGESTION

Top with toasted meringue frosting.

PROCEDURE

1. To make the crust of the pie, combine the crushed biscuits and melted butter. The mixture will have a sandy consistency.
2. Using your fingers, press down the biscuit mixture into a 9-inch pan in an even layer. Pop it into the fridge for 1 hour to set properly.
3. Meanwhile, to make the filling, bring the coconut milk or water to a slight boil.
4. Once it starts to boil, take it off the heat and add the gelatine. Stir quickly to dissolve the gelatine. Let the mixture cool and come to room temperature. It will become very thick once it cools down.
5. Add mango pulp, cream cheese, lime zest, cooled gelatine mixture and castor sugar in a blender. Blend until everything is well combined and smooth.
6. Pour the mango filling over the cooled biscuit crust. Let the pie set in the fridge for at least 2 hours.

OAT AND CHOCOLATE COOKIES

I love using oats in my baking, especially in desserts that have chocolate. If you've not tried it yet, these cookies are going to leave you pleasantly surprised.

INGREDIENTS

½ cup coconut oil or butter
½ cup lightly packed brown sugar
½ cup castor sugar
1 egg
1¼ cups rolled oats
½ cup whole-wheat flour
½ teaspoon baking soda
½ cup chocolate chips

PROCEDURE

1. In a large bowl, combine coconut oil or butter, brown sugar and castor sugar. Beat well.
2. Beat in the egg.
3. Fold in the oats. Add the wheat flour and baking soda.
4. Mix well to make sure everything is well incorporated.
5. Let the cookie dough sit in the fridge for 30 minutes.
6. Preheat the oven to 180°C.
7. On a baking tray lined with parchment paper, scoop spoonfuls of the cookie dough at equal distance.
8. Gently press them with your fingers to flatten them. Top with chocolate chips.
9. Bake at 180°C for 10-15 minutes, only until the edges are golden-brown.

EGGLESS

ORANGE TARTS

After endless disasters and experiments, I felt like an alternative-baking hero when these eggless orange tarts made with quinoa and oats finally came to life. They can beat my regular orange tarts any day. You can make them vegan by replacing butter with the same quantity of coconut oil.

TART SHELL

1 cup rolled oats

½ cup black quinoa

2 tablespoons brown sugar

4 tablespoons maple syrup

½ cup unsalted butter, melted

ORANGE CURD

½ cup water

½ cup fresh orange juice

¼ cup granulated white sugar

2 tablespoons custard powder

1 tablespoon cornflour

1 tablespoon orange zest

2 tablespoons butter, softened

PROCEDURE

1. Preheat the oven to 180°C.

2. In a food processor, combine rolled oats, quinoa and brown sugar. Process until everything is finely ground.

3. Add maple syrup and melted butter. Mix well until the dough begins to come together.

4. Press down the dough into four 2-inch tart pans or one 8-inch tart pan.

5. Let them rest in the refrigerator for 10-15 minutes.

6. Bake the tarts at 180°C for 15 minutes.

7. Meanwhile, make the filling.

8. In a large saucepan set over medium heat, cook orange juice, water and sugar until the sugar melts.

9. Add cornflour and custard powder. Mix vigorously to prevent lumps.

10. Bring the mixture to a boil. It should be thick enough to coat the back of a spoon.

11. Turn off the heat and immediately and add orange zest and butter. Mix well and make sure that the butter is completely incorporated.

12. Let the filling cool at room temperature. Fill the tart shells with the orange curd.

13. Refrigerate for at least 30 minutes before serving.

Retaining
other foot of
mouth gaping, lips
berian wolf, I slipped the
ened it and tied the knot behind
was now clamped shut and just to
plied a second bandage so th
trussed.
This was when th
confidently at the
above the enci
ly and from
ing issued.
of a thous
It was strange, but somehow the labels on
backs made them look even more pathetic;
tion mart labels stuck roughly with paste
hairy rumps, stressing the little creatures'
helpless merchandise.
As I lifted one sodden
45
was still inside the cow,
with pain but submitting
ministrations.

PEAR MUFFINS WITH PECAN CRUMBLE

I'm a firm believer of eating dessert for breakfast. Desserts like these pear muffins solidify my belief.

INGREDIENTS

¼ cup honey
¼ cup vegetable oil
½ cup Greek yogurt
2 eggs
¼ cup milk
1 cup whole-wheat flour, sifted
1 cup traditional oats
1 teaspoon cinnamon powder
¼ teaspoon ground nutmeg
4 teaspoons baking powder
1 large pear, peeled and cubed

CRUMBLE

⅓ cup traditional oats
2 tablespoons whole-wheat flour
⅓ cup pecans, roughly chopped
¼ teaspoon ginger powder
¼ cup honey

PROCEDURE

1. Preheat the oven to 200°C.
2. In a large bowl, combine honey, vegetable oil and yogurt.
3. Beat in the eggs and milk. Whisk everything together.
4. In a separate bowl, whisk together flour, oats, cinnamon powder, nutmeg and baking powder.
5. Gently fold in the dry ingredients into the wet ingredients, mixing only until everything is well combined and you do not see any flour pockets.
6. Fold in the cubed pear.
7. To make the topping, combine all the crumble ingredients in a bowl.
8. Using an ice-cream scoop, transfer the batter into a muffin pan lined with paper liners, filling two-thirds of each mould.
9. Generously sprinkle the crumble on the top.
10. Bake at 200°C for 10 minutes and then reduce the temperature to 180°C. Bake for another 20 minutes.

EGGLESS, GLUTEN FREE

ROSE CAKE

I made this cake for this New Year's Day and my family agreed that it was the best way to kickstart the year! Fragrant layers of rose cake filled with pistachio pastry cream and topped with fresh raspberries make for an elegant dessert.

ROSE CAKE

¾ cup butter, softened

1 teaspoon rose water

1 cup castor sugar

4 eggs

2 cups all-purpose flour

2 teaspoons baking powder

1 cup milk

PISTACHIO PASTRY CREAM FILLING

1 cup milk

2 egg yolks

¼ cup castor sugar

3 tablespoons corn starch

½ cup pistachio, finely ground

½ cup heavy cream, whipped to soft peaks

1 cup fresh raspberries

PROCEDURE

1. Line two 6-inch round cake pans. Preheat the oven to 180°C.

2. In a large bowl, beat the butter with rose water. Add castor sugar and beat until the mixture is light and fluffy.

3. Beat in the eggs, one at a time.

4. Fold in the flour and baking powder and mix until everything is well combined.

5. Beat in the milk.

6. Divide the batter equally into the 2 cake pans and bake for 30-40 minutes. Let them cool completely.

7. To make the pastry cream, bring the milk to a boil.

8. In a bowl, combine egg yolks, sugar and corn starch.

9. Pour the hot milk on the egg mixture in 3 batches and mix well.

10. Transfer the mixture back to the saucepan set over medium heat. Keep mixing vigorously until the pastry cream begins to thicken. Take it off the heat and let it cool completely.

11. Fold the pastry cream into the whipped cream and fold in the ground pistachios.

12. Spread a generous layer of the pastry cream filling on the cooled cake layers.

13. Top the cake with fresh raspberries.

POPCORN COOKIES

Meet the president of snack land. As someone who loves to snack, these cookies (eggless!) with popcorn, marshmallows and chocolate chunks are a dream come true. Makes 12 cookies.

INGREDIENTS

1 tablespoon ground flaxseeds
\+ **2 tablespoons** water
½ cup butter, softened
½ cup castor sugar
1 cup all-purpose flour
¼ cup cocoa powder, sifted
1 teaspoon baking soda
2 tablespoons cornflour
¼ cup milk
1 cup popped popcorn, unsalted
¼ cup dark chocolate chunks
8-10 mini marshmallows

PROCEDURE

1. In a small bowl, combine ground flaxseeds and water. Let it rest for 5 minutes. You can substitute flaxseed with a regular egg.
2. In a large bowl, beat the butter and castor sugar until the mixture is fluffy.
3. Add in the flaxseeds and egg and beat well.
4. Gently fold in the flour, cocoa powder and baking soda.
5. Beat in the milk.
6. Fold the popped popcorn into the cookie dough. Pop the dough in the fridge for 30 minutes to prevent it from spreading too much in the oven.
7. Preheat the oven to 180°C.
8. Scoop the chilled dough on a baking tray lined with parchment paper.
9. Gently press the dough with your fingers and top it with chocolate chunks and marshmallows.
10. Bake at 180°C for 10-15 minutes until the edges are crisp. Let the cookies cool on the baking tray for 10 minutes before lifting them off.

CARROT CAKE WITH CREAM-CHEESE MOUSSE

Carrot cake is my favourite cake and I usually make a rustic one with a generous layer of cream-cheese frosting. This is a more sophisticated version with a cream-cheese mousse set using gelatine. Makeovers are fun!

CAKE

1 cup whole-wheat flour
½ teaspoon baking soda
1 teaspoon baking powder
1 teaspoon cinnamon powder
½ cup + 2 tablespoons vegetable oil
1 cup castor sugar
2 eggs
1 teaspoon vanilla extract
1½ cup grated carrots
½ cup crushed walnuts + more for topping

MOUSSE

1 teaspoon gelatine powder
2 teaspoons cold water
1¼ cups milk
2 egg yolks
¼ cup castor sugar
1 cup cream cheese, softened
½ teaspoon vanilla beans

PROCEDURE

1. Preheat the oven to 180°C and line an 8-inch round cake pan with parchment paper.
2. Whisk together the flour, baking soda, baking powder and cinnamon powder.
3. In a separate bowl, beat the vegetable oil, sugar, eggs and vanilla for 5-6 minutes.
4. Fold in the dry ingredients into the wet without over-mixing, followed by the grated carrots and walnuts.
5. Transfer the batter into the cake pan and bake for 30-35 minutes or until a skewer inserted into the centre comes out clean. When baked, let the cake cool.
6. To make the mousse, sprinkle gelatine powder over cold water and let it rest on the kitchen counter.
7. Meanwhile, bring the milk to a boil.
8. In a separate bowl, combine eggs and sugar.
9. Slowly and gradually, pour the hot milk on the egg-and-sugar mixture while continuously whisking. Immediately sieve the mixture.
10. Add the gelatine and mix well. Now, beat in the cream cheese and vanilla.
11. Pour the mixture into a 15-cm ring sealed at the bottom with plastic wrap.
12. Let the mousse set in the freezer until it is firm.
13. Once it is properly set, demould it and place it on the cooled carrot cake.

FRIED BLUEBERRY PLUM CREPE POCKETS

I attended a cooking class in Indonesia where we made eggy crepes with a savoury filling and fried them. I didn't like those. So, I came back home and made my own version!

CREPES

1 cup all-purpose flour
4 tablespoons granulated sugar
2 tablespoons vegetable oil
2 eggs
1¼ cup milk
1 teaspoon vanilla extract
Vegetable oil, for frying

FILLING

1 cup plums, thinly sliced
½ cup blueberries, fresh or frozen
½ cup granulated sugar
¼ cup water
1 teaspoon lemon zest
2 teaspoons cornflour

CINNAMON SUGAR

1 cup castor sugar +
4 teaspoons cinnamon powder

PROCEDURE

1. To make the crepes, combine all the ingredients in a food processor until you get a smooth batter. Rest the batter in the fridge for 30 minutes.
2. Lightly brush a non-stick pan set over low heat with vegetable oil/butter.
3. Use a ladle to transfer ¼ cup batter to the heated pan. Quickly swirl the pan to spread the batter all the way to the edges of the pan.
4. Let it cook for 2 minutes and then flip to cook the other side until it is golden brown. Repeat.
5. To make the filling, combine plums, blueberries, sugar, water and lemon zest in a saucepan set over medium heat. Cook the mixture until the sugar melts and the fruit begins to break down.
6. Mix the cornflour in a tablespoon of water and add it to the plum-blueberry mixture. While continuously mixing, bring the filling to a boil. Take it off the heat and let it cool.
7. To make the crepe pockets, place about 2 tablespoons, filling in the centre of the crepe. Close all 4 edges of the crepes by overlapping them on one another. Secure the pocket using toothpicks.
8. Heat the oil for frying. Once hot, fry the crepe pockets carefully until they're golden-brown. Transfer them to a tray lined with paper towels and then roll them into cinnamon sugar.

COCONUT RASPBERRY CHEESECAKE TART

This is one of the first recipes I worked on for the book. It continues to be a favourite because it combines two desserts I love – tarts and cheesecakes. Now you don't have to pick one.

TART SHELL

½ cup butter

⅓ cup castor sugar

1 large egg yolk

1 cup all-purpose flour

¼ cup shredded coconut

CHEESECAKE FILLING

1 cup cream cheese, softened

¼ cup castor sugar

¼ cup heavy or sour cream

1 teaspoon lemon zest

1 egg

1 cup fresh raspberries

PROCEDURE

1. To make the base of the tart, cream the butter and sugar.

2. Beat in the egg yolk. Mix well.

3. Mix in flour and shredded coconut and beat until the dough begins to come together.

4. Press the dough into the bottom and up the sides of a 14x4.5-inch rectangular tart pan. Refrigerate for 30 minutes.

5. Preheat the oven to 200°C. Once the tart is chilled, prick it using a fork.

6. Bake for 10-15 minutes until it begins to turn golden. Remove from the oven and reduce the temperature to 180°C.

7. To make the filling, combine all the ingredients except the raspberries until the filling is smooth and well combined.

8. Pour the filling into the tart shell. Gently press the raspberries into the filling.

9. Bake the tart for 20-25 minutes or until the centre begins to set.

10. Once cooled, let the tart rest in the fridge for at least 30 minutes before serving.

SUNSHINE CAKE

When I first flipped this orange grapefruit upside-down cake, I instantly thought – it's a sunshine cake! I hope it makes you as happy as it made me.

INGREDIENTS

4 oranges
3 grapefruits
¼ cup golden syrup (or soft brown sugar)
1½ cups all-purpose flour
½ cup polenta flour (or another **½ cup** all-purpose flour)
2 teaspoons baking powder
½ teaspoons baking soda
1 tablespoon orange zest
1 cup vegetable oil
1½ cups castor sugar
4 eggs
1 teaspoon vanilla extract

PROCEDURE

1. Generously brush a 10-inch springform pan with melted butter.
2. On the bottom of the springform pan, spread an even layer of golden syrup or soft brown sugar.
3. Cut thin slices of oranges and grapefruits, about ½-inch thick, using a slicer or a knife. Remove the skin from the citrus slices. Ensure you don't break them apart.
4. Arrange the slices on the golden syrup in two layers. Keep the cake pan aside and prepare the batter. Preheat the oven to 180°C.
5. In a bowl, whisk together the all-purpose flour, polenta flour, baking powder, baking soda and orange zest.
6. In a separate bowl, beat the vegetable oil with sugar for about 5 minutes using an electric mixer.
7. Add one egg at a time and beat well after each addition. Beat in the vanilla extract.
8. Using a spatula, fold the dry ingredients into the wet. Work the batter till everything is well combined and there are no flour pockets.
9. Pour the batter on the citrus slices without disturbing their arrangement. Run a spatula on the batter to make sure it is evenly spread in the cake pan.
10. Bake at 180°C for 40-50 minutes until the top is golden-brown and a skewer inserted into the centre comes out clean. Once out of the oven, run a knife around the edges of the cake to release it from the pan.
11. After the cake has cooled completely, take it out of the cake pan and flip it upside down.

EGGLESS, REFINED-SUGAR FREE

BREAKFAST TART

If you're only going to make one recipe from this book, let it be this. I constantly questioned myself when I was baking this tart for the first time but now I can't get enough of it. Bonus – it doesn't have any refined sugar.

CRUST

1 cup rolled oats

1 cup almonds

4 tablespoons butter, melted

¼ cup honey

FILLING

¼ cup honey

1 tablespoon water

1 teaspoon gelatine powder

1½ cup Greek yogurt

¾ cup heavy cream

1 teaspoon orange zest

TOPPING

2 peaches, sliced

¼ cup water

One vanilla bean

1 sprig of thyme (optional)

PROCEDURE

1. Preheat the oven to 180°C.
2. In a blender, process the oats and almonds until they reach the consistency of a coarse flour.
3. Add in the butter and honey. Mix until the dough begins to come together.
4. Press the dough evenly into a 9-inch tart pan.
5. Bake at 180°C for 15 minutes. Let the tart shell cool completely.
6. To make the filling, sprinkle the gelatine over water and let stand until the gelatine softens.
7. In a saucepan, heat the honey slightly. Add the gelatine mixture to the honey and mix well.
8. Beat in the yogurt and orange zest.
9. In a separate bowl, beat the cream until soft peaks form. Fold the yogurt mixture into the cream.
10. Pour the filling into the cooled tart shell. Refrigerate for 1 hour or until the filling sets.
11. To make the topping, cook the peaches, water and vanilla bean together in a saucepan over medium heat. Let the peaches cook and become tender.
12. Take the filling off the heat and let it cool. Pour over the tart and garnish with thyme.

APPLE MUFFINS

This is my favourite eggless recipe in the book. I finished an entire batch of these muffins on my own and I've never loved peanut butter and apples in a dessert more.

INGREDIENTS

2 tablespoons ground flaxseeds
+ **5 tablespoons** water
2 cups all-purpose flour
2 teaspoons baking powder
½ teaspoon baking soda
1 teaspoon cinnamon powder
¼ teaspoon ginger powder
½ cup olive oil
½ cup lightly-packed brown sugar
½ cup castor sugar
1 cup milk
½ cup apples, peeled and finely diced
¼ cup traditional oats

PROCEDURE

1. Preheat the oven to 180°C. Prepare a muffin pan by lining it with muffin cups.
2. In a small bowl, combine ground flaxseeds and water. Let it rest for 5 minutes until the consistency resembles that of an egg.
3. In a medium-sized bowl, whisk to combine flour, baking powder, baking soda, cinnamon powder and ginger powder.
4. In a separate bowl, beat olive oil with brown and white sugar until the mixture is light and pale.
5. Add the flaxseed mixture and beat well again.
6. Now add the flour mixture to the wet ingredients, in three instalments, alternating with milk. Do not over-mix.
7. Fold in the diced apples.
8. Using an ice-cream scoop, scoop the batter into a prepared muffin pan. Fill two-thirds of each muffin cup. Sprinkle with traditional oats on the top.
9. Bake at 180°C for 10 minutes. Then reduce the temperature to 150°C and bake for another 20 minutes until the tops are golde- brown.

FLOURLESS CHOCOLATE PECAN BROWNIES

Brownies are the most popular dessert on my blog. This version is flourless and has some orange zest and pecans.

INGREDIENTS

1 cup dark chocolate, coarsely chopped
¼ cup butter, softened
6 egg whites
6 egg yolks
1 teaspoon baking powder
4 tablespoons cocoa powder
⅓ cup castor sugar
½ teaspoon orange zest
½ cup crushed pecans

PROCEDURE

1. Preheat the oven to 180°C. Line a 9x9-inch square tin with parchment paper.
2. In a double boiler, melt dark chocolate with butter. Set aside and let it cool.
3. In a large bowl, combine egg yolks, sugar, baking powder, cocoa powder and orange zest.
4. Add the chocolate-butter mixture and make sure everything is well combined.
5. Using an electric mixer, beat the egg whites until stiff peaks form.
6. Fold in the chocolate mixture into the egg whites gently. Add in the crushed pecans.
7. Transfer the batter into the square tin. Bake at 180°C for 40-50 minutes.

EGGLESS

CHOCOLATE PASSION FRUIT CAKE

I think of my Nani every time I whip up a chocolate cake because nothing comes close to the one she made. Her recipe is lost forever but I think she would have liked my version with passion fruit too.

CAKE

1 and **½ cups** all purpose flour
¾ cups cocoa powder
½ teaspoon baking soda
1 teaspoon baking powder
¾ cup oil
1 + ½ cups castor sugar
1 cup Greek yogurt (or curd hung over night)
½ teaspoon vanilla extract
½ cup milk

GANACHE

1 cup whipping cream
¼ cup passion fruit puree (without seeds)
2 cups milk chocolate chips (or finely chopped milk chocolate)

PROCEDURE

1. Preheat the oven to 180°C. line a 9-inch round cake pan with parchment paper.
2. Whisk cocoa, flour, salt, baking soda and baking powder into a bowl
3. In a large bowl, beat together oil and sugar until the mixture is pale and light
4. Add yogurt and mix well.
5. Beat in vanilla using mixer at low.
6. Add the flour mixture to the wet ingredients alternating with milk, starting and ending with the flour mixture. Mix only until well combined. Don't over mix.
7. Pour the batter into the pan and bake at 180°C for 40 minutes or until a skewer inserted in the centre comes out clean.

To Make the Ganache
1. In a saucepan set over medium heat, bring the cream and passion fruit puree to a boil.
2. Immediately pour the hot mixture over milk chocolate chips. Let the hot cream sit on the chocolate chips for 30-40 seconds
3. Then using a spatula, mix it until the chocolate chips melt completely and you have a smooth ganache. Let the ganache sit in the fridge until it is firm. I let it rest over night.

4. Using an electric mixer on high speed, beat the cold ganache until it whips up and gains volume.
5. Using an offset spatula, spread a generous layer of the whipped chocolate-passion fruit ganache on the chocolate cake.

REFINED-SUGAR FREE

MIXED BERRY SUMMER CAKE

Here's a cake for everyone who is as obsessed with berries as I am.

INGREDIENTS

2 cups all-purpose flour
2 teaspoons baking powder
¼ cup shredded coconut
½ teaspoon lemon zest
½ cup butter, softened
½ cup honey
2 eggs
1 teaspoon vanilla extract
⅓ cup almond milk
2 tablespoons chia seeds
1 cup mixed berries (fresh or frozen. I used strawberries, raspberries and blueberries)

PROCEDURE

1. Preheat the oven to 180°C. Generously brush a 9-inch tart pan or circular cake pan with melted butter.
2. In a bowl, combine flour, baking powder, shredded coconut and lemon zest.
3. In a separate bowl, beat the softened butter with honey. Add eggs and beat until they're well combined.
4. Beat in the vanilla extract.
5. Using a spatula, fold in the dry ingredients into the wet ingredients.
6. Slowly beat in the milk. Mix until the batter is smooth and lump-free.
7. Mix in the chia seeds.
8. Pour the batter into the prepared pan. Top the cake batter with mixed berries.
9. Bake at 180°C for 30-35 minutes or until a skewer inserted into the centre comes out clean.

EGGLESS

LEMON CUPCAKES

I tested this recipe many, many times, only because I couldn't believe that these cupcakes were so fluffy even without eggs!

CUPCAKES

2 tablespoons ground flaxseeds
4 tablespoons water
½ cup vegetable oil
1 cup castor sugar
4 tablespoons fresh lemon juice
½ cup whole milk
1½ cup all-purpose flour
2 teaspoons baking powder
1 tablespoon lemon zest
¼ teaspoon salt

CHARCOAL FROSTING

½ cup unsalted butter, softened
1½ cup icing sugar, sifted
2 tablespoons milk
3 tablespoons activated charcoal powder
2 teaspoons vanilla extract
12 blueberries, to garnish

PROCEDURE

1. Preheat the oven to 180°C. Line a cupcake tray with liners.

2. In a small bowl, combine ground flaxseeds and water. Mix well and let it rest for 5 minutes.

3. In a large bowl, beat oil and sugar until the mixture is pale. Beat in the flaxseed-and-water mixture and the lemon juice. Whisk in the milk.

4. Sift in the all-purpose flour, baking powder and salt into the wet ingredients. Using a spatula, mix the batter until it is smooth and lump-free. Mix in the lemon zest.

5. Using an ice-cream scoop, transfer the batter into the cupcake cavities, filling almost all the way to the top.

6. Bake at 180°C for 25-30 minutes or until a skewer inserted into the centre comes out clean. Let the cupcakes cool completely.

7. To make the frosting, beat the butter on high speed using an electric mixer for a couple of minutes.

8. While the mixer is still running, add the icing sugar in batches. Beat until it is well incorporated.

9. Beat in the milk and beat until the frosting is fluffy. Add the vanilla extract and charcoal powder, beat again.

10. Transfer the frosting into a piping bag attached with a large star tip. To make the swirl, start from the edge of the cupcake. While applying pressure on top of the piping bag, pipe in a steady movement around the edge of the cake and then build up into a swirl. Once you reach the end of the swirl, release the pressure and pull up quickly. Place a blueberry on top of each swirl.

NUTELLA PEANUT BUTTER COOKIES

I wanted to make Nutella cookies, but my intern wanted to bake a batch of peanut butter cookies. We could have argued but we chose to enjoy the best of both worlds.

INGREDIENTS

12 teaspoons Nutella
½ cup butter, softened
½ cup soft brown sugar
¼ cup castor sugar
¾ cup peanut butter
1 teaspoon vanilla extract
1 egg
1½ cups all-purpose flour
1 teaspoon baking soda
4 tablespoons milk, if necessary
Cocoa nibs and sea salt, to top

PROCEDURE

1. Roll Nutella into 12 small balls and place them on a tray lined with parchment paper. Refrigerate until firm.
2. In a large bowl, beat the butter with brown and castor sugar until it is fluffy.
3. Beat in the peanut butter and vanilla extract.
4. Add the egg and beat until well combined.
5. Using a spatula, fold in the all-purpose flour and baking soda.
6. If the dough is too dry, add the milk. Let the dough sit in the fridge for 30 minutes. Preheat the oven at 180°C.
7. Once the dough has chilled, roll it into balls of equal sizes. The batter will make about 12 balls.
8. Flatten them and place the firm Nutella balls on them. Wrap the peanut butter dough around the Nutella balls and gently flatten them again with your fingers. Top with cocoa nibs and sea salt.
9. Place them on a baking tray lined with parchment paper. Bake at 180°C for 10-15 minutes until the cookies are golden-brown.
10. Let them cool completely before lifting them off the baking tray.

MANGO CAKE

This cake is so pretty that it's on the book's cover! It has all the ingredients and fruits that I love, like summer on a plate.

INGREDIENTS

½ cup vegetable oil
¾ cup castor sugar
½ cup mango puree
1 teaspoon pure vanilla extract
4 eggs at room temperature
2 cups all-purpose flour
4 teaspoons baking powder

CREAM-CHEESE FROSTING

½ cup unsalted butter, softened
½ cup cream cheese, softened
1½ cups icing sugar, sifted twice
1 teaspoon cardamom powder

PROCEDURE

1. Preheat the oven to 180°C. Lightly brush a Bundt cake pan or a regular 9-inch round cake pan with butter.
2. In a large bowl, beat oil and sugar until the mixture is pale.
3. Beat in the mango puree and vanilla extract.
4. Add eggs, one at a time. Beat well after each addition.
5. Sift in the flour and baking powder. Mix until everything is well combined and the batter comes together.
6. Pour the batter into the prepared cake pan. Bake at 180°C for 30-40 minutes or until a toothpick inserted into the centre comes out clean.
7. Meanwhile, make the cream-cheese frosting. Beat the butter with cream cheese until the mixture is fluffy. Add in the icing sugar and cardamom powder.
8. Beat until the frosting is light and fluffy. Spread over the cooled mango cake.
9. Top the cake with fresh seasonal fruit and berries. I used blackberries, strawberries, passion fruit puree and nectarines.

APPLE CHOUX BUNS

Getting choux right takes some practice but once you have that trick up your sleeve, you can serve desserts as fancy as these apple cheesecake-filled choux buns dipped in toffee sauce. Don't be intimidated by the long recipe, it's easier than you think! Makes 12 small buns.

TIPS BEFORE YOU GET STARTED

1. Use salted butter for the choux. The salt prevents the choux from cracking. If you're using unsalted butter, add a pinch of salt to the water.

2. Cube the butter before adding it to the water so that it melts quickly, without too much water evaporating.

3. Add the flour to the water-butter mixture in one go. This is important so as to shock the flour. Make sure there are no large flour pockets.

4. Do not skip the step of cooking the flour mixture again. Doing so is essential because it evaporates the excess water in the dough. Use a wooden spoon to keep mixing the dough and take it off the heat when you see a layer of starch at the bottom of your pan.

5. Make sure your dough is completely cooled before you add the eggs. Adding eggs to hot dough will cook and curdle the eggs. I simply put the dough in my stand mixer attached with a paddle attachment and let it run on slow until the dough is cool. If you don't have a stand mixer, keep mixing the dough with a wooden spoon to let the hot steam escape.

6. Always add the eggs one at a time and mix well after each addition to incorporate. Once you add the eggs, the mixture may look like it is falling apart. Don't worry – just keep mixing and it will come together.

7. To test if your choux paste is at the right consistency, dip your finger in cold water and run it across the choux paste. It should form a trail that stays.

8. Once you have piped the choux, dip your finger in cold water and use it to even out the shape and smoothen the surface.

9. It is also important to bake the choux at the temperatures mentioned in the recipe. Do not open the oven door while the buns are baking otherwise they will collapse.

10. Once the choux are done, open the oven door just a little and let them cool gradually.

CHOUX BUNS

1 cup water

½ cup butter, cubed

1 cup all-purpose flour (sifted twice)

4 eggs

APPLE FILLING

¼ cup apple puree

1 teaspoon cinnamon powder

¼ cup icing sugar

½ cup cream cheese, softened

¼ cup unsweetened cream, whipped to firm peaks

12 fresh apple slices

TOFFEE SAUCE

From walnut cake recipe (Page 137).

PROCEDURE

1. Preheat oven to 200°C.

2. In a saucepan set over medium heat, bring water and butter to a boil.

3. Remove from heat and add flour in one go. Vigorously mix in the flour. The dough will begin to come together and form a ball. Make sure there are no flour pockets.

4. Immediately bring the mixture back on low heat and cook for another 3-5 minutes. You'll know it is done when you see a thin starch coating at the bottom of the pan.

5. Remove from heat and let the mixture cool completely.

6. Add eggs, one at a time, mixing well after each addition.

7. Transfer the mixture to a piping bag attached to a 1-cm round nozzle and pipe the dough into balls on baking sheet lined with parchment paper.

8. Bake for 5 minutes at 230°C. Reduce temperature to 165°C and bake for another 20 minutes until the choux are a rich brown colour.

9. To make the filling, combine apple puree, cream cheese, sugar and cinnamon. Fold it in the whipped cream. Transfer the filling to a piping bag fitted with ¼-inch pain tip. Refrigerate until ready to use.

10. Use a serrated knife to cut the choux bun in the middle. Use the piping bag to pipe a generous amount of apple cheesecake filling on the bottom choux. Place a fresh apple slice on the filling.

11. Dip the top of the choux bun in toffee sauce and place it on the apple slice to complete the dessert.

BREAKFAST ROLLS

This is a time-consuming recipe that needs you to be patient, but trust me, these fluffy and flavourful buns are worth it.

ROLLS

1 cup milk

2 teabags Earl Gray tea

½ cup granulated sugar

1½ tablespoons dry active yeast

½ cup butter, melted

3 eggs

4 + ¾ cups all-purpose flour

FILLING

¼ cup melted butter

3 cups frozen raspberries

1 cup castor sugar

2 tablespoons lemon juice

1 tablespoon corn starch

GLAZE

½ cup icing sugar

2 tablespoons milk

PROCEDURE

1. In a saucepan set over medium heat, bring the milk and teabags to a boil. This allows the flavour from the tea to infuse in the milk. Let the mixture rest until the milk is lukewarm. Discard the teabags.

2. To the lukewarm milk, add sugar and yeast. Let the mixture sit undisturbed for 10 minutes so that the yeast becomes foamy.

3. Using a stand mixer with a hook attachment or simply with your hands, mix in the melted butter and eggs.

4. With the mixer running, gradually add flour to the mixture and mix until everything is well combined and the dough comes together.

5. Transfer the dough onto the kitchen counter, lightly dusted with flour, and knead it for another 5 minutes until it is soft.

6. Transfer the dough into a bowl brushed with vegetable oil. Cover the bowl with a slightly damp cloth and let it rest in a warm place for 2 hours.

7. To make the filling, combine the ingredients in a bowl.

8. Once the dough has been well rested, transfer it back onto a lightly floured surface. Roll it out into a 15x9-inch rectangle. Spread an even layer of the raspberry filling on the dough.

9. Beginning at the 15-inch side, roll the dough into a cylinder. Cut into 12-15 slices using a knife or floss.

10. Place the rolls in an oven-safe dish. Let the rolls rest again in a warm place for another 2 hours.

11. Preheat the oven to 200°C. After the rolls have

become puffy, pop them into the oven and bake for 25-30 minutes until the rolls are golden-brown and the filling is bubbling.

12. To make the glaze, add milk to icing sugar and mix until it is smooth.

LEMON CARAMEL PEACH CAKE

Prepping for this cake takes time, but when all the elements come together, you'll feel like a kitchen hero.

CAKE

1 cup all-purpose flour
¾ cup hazelnuts, finely ground
1 teaspoon baking powder
½ teaspoon baking soda
½ cup butter, softened
1 cup condensed milk
1 teaspoon vanilla extract
¾ cup + 4 tablespoons milk

LEMON CARAMEL

1 cup granulated sugar
¼ cup water
4 tablespoons butter
3 tablespoons fresh lemon juice

HAZELNUT PRALINE

½ cup granulated sugar
1 cup hazelnuts, toasted

MASCARPONE FROSTING

1 cup heavy cream
1 cup mascarpone cheese
¼ cup icing sugar
4 large peaches, sliced

PROCEDURE

1. Preheat the oven to 180°C. Line two 6-inch cake pans with parchment paper.
2. In a bowl whisk flour, hazelnuts, baking powder and baking soda. In a separate bowl, beat the butter, vanilla and condensed milk together.
3. Add the dry ingredients to the butter-condensed milk mixture in 2 batches and alternate with milk. Carefully fold to mix everything together and mix only till there are no flour pockets in the batter.
4. Divide the batter evenly between the 2 pans. Bake at 180°C for 30-35 minutes or until a skewer inserted into the centre comes out clean. Let the cakes cool completely.
5. To make the lemon caramel, combine the water and sugar in a saucepan set over medium heat. While stirring occasionally, cook until the sugar melts completely and the mixture attains a dark amber colour.
6. Remove from the heat and whisk in the butter and lemon juice while the mixture is still hot.
7. To make the hazelnut praline, cook the granulated sugar in a saucepan set over medium heat until it is a light amber colour. Add hazelnuts to the hot sugar and stir to make sure all the hazelnuts are evenly coated. Immediately transfer the mixture to a baking tray and let it cool completely. It will harden as it cools.
8. Once the praline is cooled, break it and then process in the food processor to get a powder-like mixture.

9. To make the frosting, whip all the ingredients at high speed until the frosting is light, fluffy and voluminous.

10. To assemble the cake, spread a generous layer of frosting on one cake. Drizzle some lemon caramel and hazelnut praline. Arrange fresh peaches on top. Place the other cake on top and top it with frosting, praline and fresh peach slices.

CHEWY CHOCOLATE PECAN COOKIES

After baking almost every day for 5 years, if there is a dessert that I just cannot resist, it is these chocolate pecan cookies. I wake up in middle of the night thinking about these cookies and then I have no option but to bake a batch. This addiction is not healthy!

INGREDIENTS

1¼ cups all-purpose flour
1 tablespoon cornflour
½ teaspoon baking soda
½ cup unsalted butter, softened
½ cup lightly packed brown sugar
½ cup castor sugar
1 egg
½ cup pecans, crushed
½ cup chocolate chips
Sea salt, to top

PROCEDURE

1. In a small bowl combine all-purpose flour, cornflour and baking soda.
2. In a separate bowl, beat the butter with the brown and castor sugar.
3. Beat in the egg.
4. Fold the dry ingredients into the wet ingredients.
5. Refrigerate the cookie dough for 30 minutes.
6. Preheat the oven to 180°C.
7. Line a baking tray with parchment paper. Using an ice-cream scoop, place balls of cookie dough on the tray.
8. Bake the cookies for 5 minutes. Take the tray out and top the cookies with crushed pecans and chocolate chips.
9. Bake for another 10 minutes.

HUMMINGBIRD BUNDT CAKE

There are several theories about why a hummingbird cake is named so. I think it is because it makes you hum with happiness.

INGREDIENTS

2 cups all-purpose flour
4 teaspoons baking powder
1 teaspoon cinnamon powder
½ teaspoon ginger powder
1 cup vegetable oil
1½ cups castor sugar
6 eggs
2 teaspoons vanilla extract
½ cup mashed bananas
1 cup pineapple puree (Simply puree fresh/canned pineapple slices in a food processor)
¼ cup walnuts, roughly chopped

PROCEDURE

1. Preheat the oven to 180°C. Brush a Bundt cake pan with melted butter or vegetable oil.
2. In a bowl, whisk flour, baking powder, cinnamon and ginger powder together.
3. In a separate large bowl, beat the vegetable oil with sugar. The mixture will be pale.
4. Add one egg at a time and beat well. Mix in the vanilla extract.
5. Beat in the mashed bananas and pineapple puree.
6. Using a spatula, gently fold in the dry ingredients. Do not over-mix or it will result in a dense cake.
7. Once the batter is ready, fold in the chopped walnuts and pour the batter into the prepared Bundt pan.
8. Bake at 180°C for 40-50 minutes or until a skewer inserted into the centre comes out clean.

for
mark 25 years of

REFINED SUGAR FREE

BREAKFAST BISCOTTI

This biscotti is made with whole-wheat and buckwheat flour, sweetened with jaggery and loaded with nuts and seeds. Don't be afraid to throw in dried fruits, nuts and seeds that you have on hand.

INGREDIENTS

1 cup whole-wheat flour
⅓ cup buckwheat flour
2 teaspoons baking powder
2 eggs
⅔ cup jaggery, finely chopped
¼ cup vegetable oil
¼ cup dried cranberries
½ cup mixed nuts, coarsely chopped (I used walnuts and pistachios)
1 tablespoon chia seeds
1 tablespoon sesame seeds
1 tablespoon cucumber seeds

PROCEDURE

1. Preheat the oven to 180°C and line a loaf pan with parchment paper.
2. In a large bowl, combine whole-wheat flour, buckwheat flour and baking powder.
3. In a separate bowl, mix eggs, jaggery and vegetable oil together. Fold in the dry ingredients.
4. The batter will be very thick. Fold in the dried cranberries, dry fruits, chia seeds, sesame and cucumber seeds.
5. Transfer the batter to the prepared loaf pan. Bake at 180°C for 20 minutes until the top is golden-brown.
6. Let the loaf cool and then cut it into 3-inch-thick slices.
7. Lower the oven temperature to 150°C. Bake the biscotti for 5 minutes on each side. Let it cool completely. Be very careful when you're slicing the biscotti.

EGGLESS

BANANA HONEYCOMB CAKE

This is the first time I experimented with honeycomb and the candy-loving kid in me couldn't be happier with how well it complements the cake and the spiced-butter-cream frosting.

CAKE

2 ripe bananas
3 cups all-purpose flour
2 teaspoons baking powder
½ teaspoon salt
¾ cup vegetable oil
1½ cups castor sugar
1½ cups Greek yogurt
¾ cup milk
¼ cup crushed pecans

BUTTER-CREAM FROSTING

½ cup unsalted butter, softened
1½ cups icing sugar, sifted
1 teaspoon cinnamon powder
¼ teaspoon ginger powder
¼ teaspoon grated nutmeg
2 tablespoons milk

HONEYCOMB

1 cup castor sugar
6 tablespoons golden syrup
2 teaspoons baking soda

PROCEDURE

1. Preheat the oven to 200°C. Line a 9-inch circular cake pan with parchment paper.
2. Place 2 bananas on the baking tray and cook them in the oven for 10-15 minutes or until their skin turns black. Mash and let them cool.
3. In a bowl, whisk together flour, salt and baking powder.
4. In a large bowl, beat sugar and oil until the mixture becomes pale. Beat in the Greek yogurt and bananas.
5. Fold in the flour mixture in two batches, alternating with milk. Fold in the crushed pecan nuts.
6. Pour the batter into the prepared cake tin and bake for 40 minutes. Let it cool completely.

Frosting

1. Beat the butter with cinnamon powder, nutmeg and ginger powder on high speed using an electric mixer for a couple of minutes.
2. While the mixer is still running, add the icing sugar in batches. Beat until it is well incorporated.
3. Beat in the milk and beat until the frosting is fluffy.

Honeycomb

1. Line a 4x4-inch square pan with parchment paper.
2. In a saucepan set over medium heat, cook castor sugar and golden syrup until the sugar melts. Continue cooking until it turns into an amber colour.

3. Turn off the heat and immediately add the baking soda. The mixture will start to bubble. Give it a stir and quickly transfer the hot mixture into the baking pan.
4. Let it sit at room temperature for 30 minutes until it hardens. Break it into shards and arrange these on the cake.

EGGLESS

NECTARINE CUSTARD TART

The nectarine-blackberry galette is a special dessert because I remember making it for my first ever commissioned assignment. Here is a gluten-free version, which is equally satisfying.

FOR CRUST

1 cup buckwheat flour
¼ cup ground almonds
½ cup cold butter, cubed
4 tablespoons granulated sugar
4 tablespoons ice-cold water
1 egg+ splash of milk to brush
½ cup flaked almonds

FOR FILLING

¼ cup ground almonds
8-10 nectarines, thinly sliced
5-6 blackberries
2 tablespoons fresh lemon juice
4 tablespoons honey

PROCEDURE

1. In a food processor, combine buckwheat flour, almonds, cold butter and sugar.
2. Pulse until the mixture is coarse and crumbly. Add in the cold water and pulse until the mixture begins to hold together when pinched.
3. Flatten the dough into a disk. Wrap it in plastic wrap and refrigerate for 30 minutes.
4. To make the filling, toss the nectarines and blackberries in lemon juice and honey.
5. Preheat the oven to 200°C.
6. On a parchment, roll out the dough into a circle of about ⅛-inch thickness.
7. Leaving 1-inch borders around the edge, evenly spread the ground almonds on the rolled-out dough.
8. Arrange the nectarine slices and blackberries on the layer of ground almonds.
9. Fold the edges of the galette over the fruit.
10. Generously brush the overlapped edges with egg wash. Sprinkle flaked almonds on the edges.
11. Bake at 200°C for 40-45 minutes or until the crust is completely cooled.
12. Let it cool on the baking tray completely before lifting. Serve with vanilla ice cream.

ORANGE AND CUSTARD PAVLOVAS

Honestly, I'm not a pavlova fan but these mini pavlovas are delightful. If you make them in advance, store them in an airtight container.

MERINGUE

4 egg whites

2 cups castor sugar

½ teaspoon vanilla extract

2 teaspoons corn starch

CUSTARD

2 cups whole milk, divided

3 tablespoons custard powder

¼ cup castor sugar

½ teaspoon cardamom powder

TOPPING

8-10 sections of oranges and blood oranges

¼ cup castor sugar

6 tablespoons crushed pistachios

PROCEDURE

1. Preheat the oven to 150°C. On a parchment sheet, draw six 4-inch circles. Reverse the parchment sheet and place it on a baking tray.

2. In a stand mixer, beat the egg whites until they double in volume.

3. While the mixer is still running, gradually add sugar and beat until the egg whites are glossy and form stiff peaks.

4. Fold in the vanilla extract and corn starch.

5. Transfer the meringue on the parchment paper within the drawn circles. Bake for 1 hour and let the meringue cool once it's baked completely.

6. To make the custard, mix in the custard powder into ½ cup milk.

7. In a saucepan set over medium heat, bring the custard mixture, sugar, cream and the remaining 1½ cups milk to a boil until the custard thickens. Refrigerate for at least 1 hour.

8. To make the topping, combine citrus sections and sugar in a saucepan over low heat. Cook until the citrus sections release juices.

9. To assemble the pavlova, top the meringue with custard and citrus. Sprinkle with crushed pistachios.

LEMON-BLUEBERRY LOAF

This is my favourite loaf cake recipe and is meant for days when you want something simple but delicious.

INGREDIENTS

1½ cups all-purpose flour
2 teaspoons baking powder
½ teaspoon baking soda
1 teaspoon lemon zest
½ cup vegetable oil
1 cup castor sugar
3 eggs
2 tablespoons fresh lemon juice
½ cup whole milk
½ cup fresh blueberries

PROCEDURE

1. Preheat the oven to 180°C. Line an 9x4-inch loaf pan with parchment paper.
2. In a bowl, combine flour, baking powder, baking soda and lemon zest.
3. In a separate bowl, beat vegetable oil and sugar together.
4. Add eggs, one at a time, and beat well after each addition. Beat in the lemon juice.
5. In three batches, gently fold the dry ingredients into the wet ingredients alternating with milk. Make sure not to over-mix the batter.
6. Fold in the blueberries.
7. Pour the batter into the prepared loaf pan.
8. Bake at 180°C for 30-40 minutes or until a skewer inserted into the centre comes out clean.

RED GRAPE AND APPLE YEAST CAKE

Yeast cakes are slightly more time-consuming than regular ones but when you take the first bite you know it is worth the time you put in.

INGREDIENTS

½ cup milk
2½ teaspoons dry yeast
½ cup castor sugar
½ cup vegetable oil
2 eggs
2 cups all-purpose flour
1 tablespoon orange zest
1 cup red grapes
1 apple, thinly sliced
¼ cup whole pecans
8-10 dried cranberries
¼ cup lightly packed brown sugar
¼ teaspoon ginger powder

PROCEDURE

1. Warm the milk and sprinkle yeast on top. Set aside and let it sit for 5 minutes.
2. In a large bowl, combine sugar and vegetable oil.
3. Add the eggs and beat well.
4. Fold in the all-purpose flour and orange zest.
5. Add the milk-yeast mixture and mix until well combined.
6. Transfer the batter to a lightly buttered 8-inch round springform pan.
7. Let the batter rest in a warm place for 1 hour.
8. Meanwhile, toss the red grapes, apples, pecans and cranberries in brown sugar and ginger powder.
9. Preheat the oven to 200°C.
10. Place the fruit on top of the cake batter.
11. Bake at 200°C for about 40-50 minutes until the cake rises and is cooked through.
12. Cool completely before demoulding. Serve with whipped cream.

EGGLESS

WALNUT CAKE

In my opinion, a slice of this eggless walnut cake would make for a great company on a cold day. The dense cake with yogurt-maple frosting and pears cooked in toffee sauce is basically like a warm hug.

CAKE

2 cups all-purpose flour
2 teaspoons baking powder
½ teaspoon cinnamon powder
¼ teaspoon ginger powder
½ cup walnut butter (Process the walnuts in the food processor until you get walnut butter.)
½ cup unsalted butter, softened
1 cup castor sugar
½ cup Greek yogurt
1 cup milk

YOGURT FROSTING

½ cup Greek yogurt
½ cup heavy cream, whipped to soft peaks
4 tablespoons maple syrup

TOFFEE SAUCE PEARS

½ cup butter, softened
½ cup lightly packed brown sugar
½ cup fresh cream
1 cinnamon stick
4 pears, peeled and sliced

PROCEDURE

1. Preheat the oven to 180°C. Line an 8-inch cake pan with parchment paper.
2. In a bowl, combine flour, baking powder, cinnamon and ginger powder.
3. In a separate bowl, beat walnut butter, regular butter and sugar together until the mixture is light and fluffy. Add yogurt and mix well.
4. Add dry ingredients to wet ingredients in 3 batches while alternating with milk. Do not over mix. Mix only until everything is well combined and you don't see any flour pockets.
5. Pour the batter into the prepared cake pan and bake at 180°C or until a skewer inserted into the centre comes out clean. Let the cake cool completely.
6. To make the frosting, fold the yogurt and maple into the whipped cream. Generously spread on the cooled walnut cake.
7. To make the toffee sauce pears, cook the butter and sugar in a skillet set over medium heat. Add the pear slices and the cinnamon stick. Let the mixture come to a simmer.
8. Remove the pear slices and cinnamon stick. Add the cream to the butter-sugar mixture and bring it to a boil.
9. Then take it off the heat and add the pears back to the mixture. Once cooled completely, pour the toffee sauce and the pears on the cake.

GLUTEN FREE

PLUM CAKE

When I started working on this recipe, I was prepared for a disaster. To my surprise, it made for a perfect tea cake.

INGREDIENTS

1 cup jowar flour
2 teaspoons baking powder
1 cup almond flour
½ teaspoon cinnamon powder
¼ teaspoon ginger powder
½ cup olive oil
1 cup light brown sugar
¼ cup milk
4 eggs
10-12 plums, sliced
½ cup almonds, flaked

PROCEDURE

1. Preheat the oven to 180°C and line a 9x9-inch square pan with parchment, leaving edges to make handles on two sides. This makes it easier to lift the cake.
2. Combine jowar, almond flour, baking powder, cinnamon and ginger powder in a bowl so that everything is well combined. Set aside.
3. In a separate bowl, beat olive oil and sugar together.
4. Beat in the eggs, one at a time.
5. Use a spatula to fold the dry ingredients into the wet ingredients. Mix in the milk.
6. Pour the batter into the prepared cake pan.
7. Arrange plum slices on the batter and sprinkle flaked almonds on top.
8. Bake at 180°C for 25-30 minutes or until a wooden skewer inserted in the centre comes out clean.

EGGLESS

LEMON-STRAWBERRY SHORTCAKES

This classic dessert is reminiscent of the endless servings of strawberry and cream I had as a kid. Only better!

INGREDIENTS

2 cups all-purpose flour
1 teaspoon baking powder
½ teaspoon baking soda
½ teaspoon lemon zest
4 tablespoons castor sugar
1 tablespoon lemon juice
1 + 1½ cups whipping cream
2 cups strawberries, diced
6 tablespoons castor sugar
¼ cup castor sugar
Beans from one vanilla pod

PROCEDURE

1. Preheat the oven to 200°C.
2. In a large bowl, whisk together the flour, baking powder, baking soda, lemon zest and castor sugar.
3. Add lemon zest and whipping cream. Mix well until everything is well combined. The dough will be wet and sticky.
4. Using an ice-cream scoop, scoop the dough into balls, 1-inch apart, on a baking tray lined with parchment paper.
5. Bake at 200°C for 15-20 minutes until they're golden-brown.
6. Meanwhile, drizzle 6 tablespoons of sugar over the diced strawberries and let it rest for 15 minutes until the strawberries become juicy.
7. Using an electric mixer, beat 1 cup whipping cream with vanilla on high speed. While the mixer is still running slowly add castor sugar. Beat until the cream forms soft peaks.
8. To assemble the cakes, place a generous amount of strawberries on the shortcakes.
9. Top with a dollop of whipped cream. Refrigerate for 30 minutes before serving.

RASPBERRY-QUINOA MUFFINS

I was making regular raspberry muffins when I saw cooked quinoa lying on my kitchen counter. I decided to add an entire cup to my batter and I've never been happier with a crazy idea. Talk about packing protein in your dessert!

INGREDIENTS

⅓ cup vegetable oil
½ cup castor sugar
3 eggs
1 teaspoon vanilla extract
⅓ cup + 4 tablespoons milk
1 cup cooked quinoa, cooled
1 cup whole-wheat flour
4 teaspoons baking powder
½ cup fresh raspberries
¼ cup almond flakes

NOTE To cook quinoa, bring 2 cups of water to a boil. Add 1 cup quinoa to the boiling water. Reduce the heat to low and cover the pot. Cook for 15 minutes. Let the quinoa cool completely.

PROCEDURE

1. Preheat the oven to 180°C. Line a muffin pan with parchment or brush generously with melted butter.
2. In a large bowl, combine oil and sugar. Add eggs and mix well.
3. Beat in the vanilla extract. Add milk and mix well.
4. In a separate bowl, combine whole-wheat flour, quinoa and baking powder.
5. Fold in the dry ingredients into the wet ingredients.
6. Fold in the raspberries.
7. Using an ice-cream scoop, scoop the batter into the muffin pan, filling two-thirds of the cavity.
8. Top with flaked almonds.
9. Bake the muffins at 180°C for 15 minutes. Reduce the temperature to 150°C and bake for another 20 minutes.

MINI MULBERRY CAKES

When I was five years old, I spent a year in Dehradun. The huge mulberry tree in our backyard was the beginning of my love affair with mulberries and these cakes are just another expression of that love.

INGREDIENTS

½ cup butter, softened
½ teaspoon ground star anise
1 teaspoon vanilla extract
1 cup castor sugar
¼ cup sour cream
3 eggs
½ cup milk
2 cups all-purpose flour
2 teaspoons baking powder
½ cup fresh mulberries

PROCEDURE

1. Preheat the oven to 180°C and generously brush 12 mini cake pans with melted butter.
2. Beat the butter, star anise, vanilla and castor sugar until the mixture is fluffy.
3. Beat in the sour cream and the eggs. Mix well.
4. Whisk in the milk.
5. Using a spatula, fold in the all-purpose flour and baking powder. Mix only until there are no flour pockets in the batter.
6. Carefully fold in the fresh mulberries.
7. Transfer the batter into prepared cake pans and bake at 180°C for 25-30 minutes until the cakes are golden-brown and a skewer inserted into the centre comes out clean.

EGGLESS

BLUEBERRY CRUMB BARS

I added this recipe to the book at the last minute because I realized that there are days when you want dessert but you've had enough of cakes, cupcakes or even tarts. For all such days, you need these eggless blueberry bars.

CRUST AND TOPPING

2 cups all-purpose flour
1 cup rolled oats
1 teaspoon baking powder
½ cup honey
1 cup castor sugar
1 cup cold butter, cubed

BLUEBERRY FILLING

4 cups blueberries, frozen
½ cup castor sugar
1 tablespoon cornflour
1 teaspoon lemon zest

PROCEDURE

1. Preheat the oven to 180°C. Line a 9x13-inch rectangular cake pan with parchment paper, leaving excess on both the sides.
2. In a bowl, combine flour, oats, sugar, baking powder and honey. Use your fingers to incorporate the cold butter into the dough.
3. Press down half the dough evenly into the bottom of the prepared pan.
4. To make the filling, in a separate bowl, combine blueberries, sugar, cornflour and lemon zest.
5. Transfer the filling onto the crust. Crumble the remaining dough over the filling.
6. Bake at 180°C for 30-40 minutes or until the crumb is golden-brown.
7. Let it cool completely before cutting the bars.

CREAM-CHEESE CITRUS TARTS

If there was a beauty pageant for tarts, I'm sure these would win! And they taste better than they look.

TART SHELL

6 tablespoons butter, softened

¼ cup castor sugar

1 egg yolk

1 cup all-purpose flour

CREAM-CHEESE FILLING

2 cups cream cheese, softened

½ cup castor sugar

1 tablespoon fresh orange zest

8-10 sections of orange

8-10 sections of blood oranges

Beans from one vanilla pod

PROCEDURE

1. To make the tart shell, beat the butter with sugar until the mixture is smooth. Add the egg yolk and mix well.

2. Mix in the flour and beat until everything is well incorporated and the dough begins to come together.

3. Use your fingers to press down the dough into the bottom and up the sides of one 9-inch or four 4.75-inch tart pans. Refrigerate the tart shells for one hour.

4. Preheat the oven to 190°C. Use a fork to prick the completely chilled tart shells.

5. Bake the tart shells for 10 minutes or until they're golden-brown. Let them cool completely.

6. To make the filling, beat the cream cheese with castor sugar until the filling is smooth and fluffy.

7. Mix in the vanilla beans and orange zest.

8. Fill the cooled tart shells with the cream-cheese filling. Arrange the sections of oranges and blood oranges on the tarts.

CHEESECAKE

There are a few things we all need in life, one being a foolproof cheesecake recipe.

BASE

1¼ cup Oreo biscuits, crushed

¼ cup melted butter

FILLING

1½ cups cream cheese, softened

1 cup mascarpone cheese, softened

1 cup whipping cream

½ cup castor sugar

3 eggs

CHOCOLATE GANACHE

1 cup dark chocolate, coarsely chopped

½ cup fresh or heavy cream

PROCEDURE

1. Preheat the oven to 180°C.

2. In a bowl, combine crushed Oreo biscuits and melted butter. Press the mixture into an 8-inch springform pan. Bake at 180°C for 10 minutes.

3. Meanwhile, to make the filling, slowly beat the cream cheese, mascarpone cheese, whipping cream and sugar together until everything is well combined. Don't whip the ingredients too much. The idea is to not incorporate air. If you don't have mascarpone cheese, you may replace it with an equal quantity of sour cream.

4. Add eggs, one at a time, and mix just until blended. Overmixing the batter will incorporate too much air into it, which is not desirable. The mixture should be smooth and lump-free.

5. Pour the filling on the baked Oreo base. Place the springform pan in a water bath and pop it into the oven. Reduce the temperature to 150°C and bake for 1 hour.

6. You know the cheesecake is done when the edges begin to puff, the cake is almost set and the centre is still jiggly. Do not insert a toothpick to test its doneness.

7. Once the cheesecake is baked, let it cool for 15 minutes. Run the knife around the edges to release it and let it cool completely while it's still in the pan.

8. Once the cheesecake is at room temperature, take it out of the cake pan and let it rest in the fridge for at least 5 hours or overnight.

9. To make the chocolate ganache, bring the cream to a simmer either in the microwave or in a double boiler.

10. Immediately pour the hot cream on the chopped chocolate. Let it sit for 2 minutes.
11. Using a spatula, mix until the chocolate melts completely and you get a smooth ganache. Let it cool.
12. Pour the ganache on the cheesecake. Decorate with chocolate shavings.

VEGAN ORANGE CAKE

Made using easily available ingredients, this cake is a delight to bake and to eat. I baked it in a Bundt pan but you can use the same recipe to make a loaf or a simple circular cake.

INGREDIENTS

2 cups all-purpose flour
1 teaspoon baking powder
1 teaspoon baking soda
1 tablespoon orange zest
½ cup brown sugar
½ cup organic white sugar
½ cup fresh orange juice
½ cup vegetable oil
¾ cup hot water
¼ cup almonds, flaked
A pinch of salt

PROCEDURE

1. Preheat the oven to 180°C and prepare a Bundt pan.
2. In a medium-sized bowl, whisk to combine flour, baking powder, baking soda, salt and orange zest.
3. In a large bowl, combine both the sugars, orange juice, vegetable oil and water.
4. Add the dry ingredients to the wet ingredients. Fold to combine. Do not over-mix.
5. Pour the batter into the tin. Top with flaked almonds.
6. Bake at 180°C for 30-40 minutes or until a skewer inserted in the cake comes out clean.

STYLING

The dessert is ready, it's time to dress it up and make it look like a masterpiece.

STYLE WITH SHIVESH

As a food blogger, it is very important for me to not only bake delicious desserts but also make sure I style and photograph them well. Like me, there are so many other people who run recipe blogs and websites. A lot of us also run our businesses online and displaying a pretty product on the show window (the internet in our case) is very important to get the customer to come in. If your product doesn't look great, there'll be less people willing to taste it. I've also realized that most people pick a recipe to try out which has a better-looking picture with it over the one that doesn't. Even on social media, everyone might not be able to taste your desserts but they do consume them with their eyes. In such situations, styling and photographing desserts, or food in general, becomes important.

While a lot of us are comfortable whipping up a dessert in the kitchen, it is the styling and photographing that intimidates us. This happens largely because we imagine it being done in studios by professionals who own the fanciest equipment. Let me pop that bubble for you. To style and photograph your food beautifully, all you need is a basic set-up and equipment, some tricks up your sleeve and a lot of understanding of what you're shooting. I'm going to take you through the process of creating a beautiful frame and share some tips and tricks along the way.

FOOD-STYLING TIPS

FOOD IS THE STAR

Remember, you're styling the dessert and that is what should shine in the picture. Your entire composition should be centred on the food. Make sure your frame does not have any elements that take attention away from the star of your picture. When you're composing your picture, start by first placing your food in the frame. Once that is in place, you can build the picture by placing other elements around it and see what complements the food and what doesn't. In all situations, your food must be the first thing that catches the eye of the viewer. To ensure this, make sure all other elements in your picture are smaller than the dessert or the food you're styling.

DRESS UP YOUR FOOD RIGHT

You need to make sure the food is dressed right. While prepping the food, use the freshest and the best quality ingredients. It makes a lot of difference to how the final product ends up looking. It is also very important to garnish your food and dress it up properly, without going overboard. It could be drizzling your pear muffins with some white chocolate (Page 71) or decorating the Eton mess cake with edible flowers (Page 58). Once you get the look of your dessert right, you win half the battle! If your dessert isn't dressed up properly or is overdone, it is hard to fix even with the prettiest props.

CUT AND SHOOT

After shooting the whole dessert, I always try and take a few shots after cutting a slice of the dessert or taking a bite. It gives the viewer a peek into what the texture of the dessert is like and how it looks from the inside. Make sure your slice/bite is neat and doesn't end up making the food look unappetizing.

MESSY IS GOOD, DIRTY IS NOT

Every food stylist has their own style. While some people like to keep their frame completely clean, others like me usually play around and create a little mess in the frame. It adds movement to the frame and I personally thinks it makes

your composition more relatable. Some crushed nuts here and there, some crumbs of the cake, a melting scoop of ice cream or a splatter of chocolate make the frame more fun and real. Your frame doesn't have to be flawless. However, there is a thin line between messy and dirty. While messy is good, you don't want to push it towards being dirty. Something like an oil stain or too much spilling will only look dirty.

DO NOT OVERDO IT

Food styling is all about knowing when to stop. At times, we might end up going overboard and ruin a frame that was almost perfect before we added another half-a-dozen elements. You may have ten pretty props or interesting elements that would look great in the frame with food, but you don't need to add all of them in a single frame. How do you know when to stop? Once you feel that the first thing that you notice in the frame is not the food, you probably need to declutter. If you're adding flowers in the frame, make sure you're only adding one variety. If you're adding milk bottles, don't place more than a couple of them. Another related tip would be to not overthink. When you're styling food, you need to go with the flow and see what looks good there. Having a concept in mind is great but overthinking while you're adding elements to your frame can be a bad idea. Your composition might end up looking choreographed or staged.

ADD FRESHNESS

It's always a good idea to pack your composition with as many fresh elements as you can. I love adding fresh fruits and flowers to my pictures. I also get saplings of fruit plants from the nursery, which add so much freshness to a frame. Since the last two winters, I've been growing strawberries at home. The strawberry plant makes for such a great addition to a strawberry dessert shoot. Besides that, I also have a mulberry plant, a Chinese orange plant as well as a peach plant. If you're adding fresh fruit, make sure you slice it right before you take the pictures because you'll lose out on all the freshness if the fruits sit around for too long – apples and pears become brownish, citrus fruits like oranges and lemons begin to form a film on them and even stone fruits like peaches and plums start looking dull. Another way to add freshness to your composition is by using herbs. Garnishing a dessert with herbs like thyme, rosemary, mint or sage adds life to your frame. Keep your herbs soaked in cold water until right before you add them to the frame. This helps lock the freshness and colour. Adding plants and flowers to your frame is another way of bringing in some freshness to your composition. If I'm shooting a strawberry dessert, I sneak in a tiny strawberry plant that I have into the frame. Similarly, adding a few branches and leaves from a lemon tree for a dessert that has lemon does the trick for me. I try not using plastic in my images (although I use this particular bunch of artificial flowers because they look very real in pictures). Plastic trays, plates, straws, baskets do not look good in pictures. Whenever I look at a food composition with plastic in it, it seemed to suck the freshness out of the frame and made it look very artificial. Look for alternatives to plastic elements. You could use paper straws instead of plastic ones and wooden/tin boxes instead of plastic baskets.

I also love adding edible flowers on my desserts. If my dessert looks like it is missing something, I simply garnish it with a few edible flowers that I grow in my balcony. They add not only freshness but also colour

to the picture. Pansies, orchids, calendulas, nasturtiums, violas, dianthus are some edible flowers that I love using when I'm styling pictures. A lot of these are available in markets and big departmental stores but I like to grow mine at home.

ADD, REMOVE, START OVER AGAIN

When you're building up your frame, don't be too rigid. Sometimes we have an image in mind but when we try and replicate it, it does not translate into what we had imagined. At this point, be open-minded enough to make changes or scrap off that image from your head completely. As you go on to add elements to your frame, you'll see some things seem to work while others do not. It is important to keeping removing elements that don't work and adding newer ones. Be flexible and also try changing the positions of your props. Even if you think a set-up works, take a few pictures and move things around again and you may land up on a better composition. If you're not happy with the frame at all, don't be afraid to wipe the canvas clean and start over again. Sometimes if I think I'm stuck or things just don't seem to fall in place, I clear the space completely and take a five-minute break. Then I start again with a fresh concept and idea.

EXPERIMENT

As a food stylist, it is very important to try new things and constantly reinvent yourself, while sticking to the style that is truly yours. Your style would be something that you enjoy doing the most. I used to take bright pictures for the longest time before I found creative satisfaction in taking moody pictures. I don't stick to taking just dark pictures now, but that is the style I enjoy doing more. Over the years, you'll subconsciously develop a style that your viewers will identify and associate with you. If they look at your work, they will be able to say that it's yours without being told.

However, having a trademark style must not stop you from being creative or trying your hand at new techniques. As a stylist, it is very easy to get comfortable with the same few compositions and framing techniques. Food styling can become boring for you and your viewers if it is repetitive. Try and push boundaries and attempt new things. What I've also realized is that when you're not challenging yourself, you end up composing pictures that look staged or forced. There was a point, right before I started working on the book, where I realized that most of my styling was using just two boards. That is when I decided to step out of my comfort zone and style my desserts in different places, like by the window or in a wooden crate. You know your style is getting repetitive when you get too comfortable with it.

Tickle your mind every single time before you begin styling and make a conscious decision to attempt something fresh. You may not be equally happy with the results but honestly, if it is not challenging, it's not fun. Food styling is all about having fun. You need to enjoy the process to translate that in the final image.

Self-doubt is a part of any creative process. We all go through phases where we begin to question our work and think it's not good enough. While some self-analysis is great, and might get you to improve your work, self-doubt usually only holds you back. It pushes you into a zone where you don't feel confident enough to do your job. Food styling requires you to work with an open mind, some confidence and to have fun. That can only happen when you kick self-doubt away.

PRACTISE

Food styling is not something you can get the hang of in a day. Consider the image on the right. It includes all the elements I've written about and it took me several hits and misses to get the waffle-to-fruit ratio just right. So, keep practising. Try and style something every day and you'll see that your compositions will get better and you will feel more confident in moving things around while setting up.

THE SET-UP

My set-up for food styling and photography is simple. I shoot in my home at a spot that gets a good amount of natural light. I don't use any expensive equipment. You can easily replicate this in your home/studio. My basic set-up usually consists of two boards (read the section on backgrounds), one camera and a tripod. I don't use any studio lights or reflectors or diffusers, but I don't discourage you from using these. You may look at this image of the caramel pecan pie on the left to understand the tips that follow. It has the right background, mood, props, fabric, texture and lighting.

SELECT THE MOOD OF THE PHOTO

It is very important to pick the treatment that you'd like to give your pictures because your entire styling is dependent on that. Will the picture be bright and white or would you like it to be dark and moody? The treatment of the picture can, but must not always, depend on the dessert you're shooting. While a summery berry tart may inspire you to style against lighter backgrounds with pastel props, it could look equally tempting against a rustic background that offers a great contrast and allows your dessert to pop. Take your time and imagine the dessert you're shooting in different settings and then take the decision of which direction you want to go.

NARRATE A STORY

This is an essential aspect of food styling. When I say narrate a story, I don't mean that your pictures should have a plot in them. It only means that all the elements of your picture should seamlessly come together to create an interesting frame. One way of doing this is to try and think of a theme for your picture. This is not always possible but you could always have a scenario in mind. Is it a breakfast scene? Is the dessert being eaten for tea? Is it a dessert you'd take for a picnic? The buckwheat biscotti (Page 119) could be something you eat for breakfast or with your afternoon tea, hence the newspaper and the teacup in the frame. Once you have a theme in mind, you will style all the elements in a way that nothing looks random, forced or out of place.

PICK THE RIGHT BACKGROUND

As a food stylist, picking the right background is a crucial decision and getting that wrong can bring down your picture. I personally love using natural surfaces as backgrounds. A rustic wood background for my moody pictures and a slab of white marble for my brighter pictures are my go-to picks. Old furniture, worn-out baking trays and painted walls also make for good backgrounds.

I once asked my carpenter to collect some old wood and join it together to make me a background. I use this all the time. Make sure you don't use wood that is smooth and looks perfect. You want wood with a weathered look. Its grooves and roughness will add texture to your composition, preventing it from looking flat or one dimensional. A polished wooden background is a big no-no because it'll reflect light and not create the shadows.

I also know of stylists who use wallpapers as photography backgrounds. It is a great idea because you have a vast variety that you can pick from. They're also very easy to store and carry around.

Concrete is also an option. It adds a lot of texture and moodiness to the image.

I also use a few artificial backgrounds painted especially for food photography. There are several online stores, like Madras Prop Store, that sell customized food photography backgrounds. I also like to paint mine at home because it is easy, fun and cost effective. While picking a background, make sure it has some texture that adds a lot of element to your photo. A plain background may end up looking dead, doing nothing for your composition. At the same time, ensure that the background is not too distracting.

ADD LAYERS, TEXTURES AND HEIGHT AND DEPTH

A lot of times, even a well-styled picture can end up looking one dimensional. An interesting way to bring your pictures alive is by adding layers, textures and heights to

DO IT YOURSELF

To make your own food photography background, all you need is an MDF board, a couple of sponges and acrylic emulsion paints. I usually pick a couple of different shades of the same colour instead of using just one because that ends up looking too flat. I blend the colours using a sponge, which allows me to incorporate a lot of texture. Avoid overmixing, only dab and blend. Once the colours on your board have dried completely, use a sandpaper to give the background a distressed look. While selecting colours for your board, try going for a neutral colour palette. I love using greys and whites because these colours allow the food to stand out. Again, avoid overdoing the background.

the photo. Whenever you're building your frame, take a moment to check if you're adding these variations to the image. While composing your frame, make sure all the elements are placed at different distances from the camera. By doing this, you add depth to your picture and prevent it from looking flat and boring. If everything is arranged in a single line, it ends up looking very staged and artificial. Push a few props to the back and bring some forward for a more natural feel to the frame.

You must also add props of different heights to make your frame interesting. A few flat dishes along with tall bottles and a couple of stacked plates bring in a contrast of heights which will instantly make your composition look better. Needless to say, push the taller props like milk bottles to the back and let smaller elements like spoons be closer to the camera.

It is always a great idea to add layers between your dessert and the background. It lifts your dessert and helps bring more attention to it. I don't always do this, but doing so makes sure the frame doesn't look dull or lifeless. To add layers to your composition you could use fabric, burlap, baking paper, multiple plates or crushed newspaper. Making these conscious efforts will take your picture a long way.

FABRIC

Using fabric is an easy way to fill up the frame and add layers to your composition. Fabrics, if used nicely, add an element of movement in the frame and, in a way, help connect all the elements together. I usually use a piece of fabric coming in from a corner or under the plate with the dessert on it. I sometimes also use not one but two pieces of fabric in a composition if it doesn't look too cluttered. Selecting the fabric for your food compositions is tricky and you need to choose right for it to do wonders for your composition.

Keep these tips in mind:

1. Don't pick a fabric with a very bright colour. While fabrics are a good way of adding a pop of colour to the frame, you don't want a bright red or green taking away all the attention from other important elements. Go for subtle shades. The fabric colours I most frequently use are beige, white, cream, baby pink and grey.

2. Pick a fabric with solid texture. Stay away from shiny and shimmery fabrics or those with too many prints or patterns. You ideally want the fabric to look like a kitchen towel and not something you'd wear to a party.

3. Don't select something that is too thin. For styling, you want a fabric that has body to it. You should be able to create waves and movement in the fabric. If the fabric is too thin, it'll not be able to hold the waves and will fall flat. At the same time, if it is too thick, you will not be able to alter

its movement easily. I prefer using linen because it holds the structure perfectly and has an ideal texture. I also often use muslin cloth. Although it is thin, its texture is very interesting and looks great in images.

While adding fabric to your frame, use your hands carefully to give it a structure in the most natural-looking way. Instead of looking choreographed, it should look like something that was simply sitting close to the dessert. To give a more natural look to the fabric, you could simply crumple it for more texture. You could also experiment with a variety of other fabrics. Denim looks fantastic in pictures and also adds colour and texture. When I'm styling something like a hot chocolate or a dessert with cosy flavours like the date and walnut cake in this book, I'll throw in a woollen sweater to add to the cosy vibe.

Just like your props, start building your collection of fabrics as well. It is always better to have a few handy to see what colour and texture complements the food the most.

HUMAN ELEMENT

When you're composing a frame and feel like you can't find enough props to make the composition interesting, add a human element to your picture. Doing this brings life into your frame and makes your food look more accessible. In most cases, it is a hand or a pair of hands. It could be a hand holding a cup of coffee or someone with a fork in their hand going for a slice of the cake. This works the best when you're shooting a flat lay. If you're shooting a big community dessert or composing a frame where there are multiple servings, you could also have a couple of hands coming into the frame instead of just one.

Another way of adding a human element is to have a person stand behind the table and take a front-angle shot. The person in the frame could be doing an action like pouring something on the dessert, sprinkling sugar on it, frosting a cake or simply holding the dessert. Please remember that despite having a person in the frame, your dessert is the subject that still needs to be in focus. The human element in your frame must not be in focus or take away attention from your dessert. The person in the frame with the food must be dressed in bold colours that are not too bright. If the clothes have a lot of patterns, it will become too distracting. Another thing to ensure is that the clothes should not be shiny or have distracting or fluorescent colours. Anything that grabs too much attention is a big no. While selecting the colour of the clothes, which in this case becomes the background for the dessert, try going for something that is in contrast with the dessert. For example, for a white panna cotta, a dark blue shirt works because it makes the panna cotta pop.

PROPS

SELECTING THE PROPS

Props help you build a story and make the frame interesting. While I prefer going for completely clean and minimalist styling at times, I've realized that I gravitate towards photos with more props. Keep in mind that props are like the supporting cast of a movie. They're crucial since they can make or break the frame, but they should ideally not overpower your star, the food.

The props that feature in food pictures are plates, bowls and cutlery. Adding cutlery to your frame makes the food accessible and the photograph doesn't seem staged. When you're selecting a plate or a cake stand for your dessert, please ensure that it is slightly bigger than your dessert but not too big. You should be able to see about an inch of the plate around your dessert. The plate should be simple, not have too much design on it and should be of a neutral colour. Besides that, ingredients that have been used in the recipe make for great elements to fill up the space with. They're also excellent indicators of the flavours of your food. I almost always keep the fruits used in the dessert in the frame. If the recipe calls for cinnamon, include cinnamon sticks in the frame. Similarly, if you've used pecans in your dessert, break a few of them and scatter them around. I also sometimes use fresh flowers, old pictures, vintage cameras, glass jars, wooden chopping boards, milk bottles and old books. Be creative and fun while selecting the props but make sure to not overdo it.

An important question to ask while adding props is how many are too many? If you go overboard, you might end up overcrowding your frame, taking away from the beauty of the dessert. Make sure your frame is neat. Sometimes when there is too much going on, the viewer gets confused as to what is being highlighted in the picture. It is important to maintain visual hierarchy.

While selecting your props, keep a few things in mind:

1. Make sure the props are not shiny. If the prop you've picked up is shiny, it'll reflect light into the camera which will distract the viewer. I always try and select ceramic plates and bowls because their finish looks great in pictures. Besides ceramics, enamelware, stoneware and wooden props also work well. If you're putting metal props in the frame, make sure they're dull. I also stay away from plastic plates and bowls as I'm not a fan of their artificial finish.

2. The props should complement the mood that you've selected for the picture. A rustic metal bowl will look out of place if the rest of the set-up is clean and bright. Similarly, a white plate will take away too much attention if everything else in the frame is dark and moody.

3. Ensure that the props you're adding to your frame don't overshadow the food. The props shouldn't be too big.

4. Always keep in mind that the props should be relevant to the scene you're creating. A lot of times, we may end up adding things to a frame where they're not needed. I've made the mistake of keeping forks in a frame with croissants. While the vintage forks were pretty, they ended up looking odd when kept with a dessert that you don't need a fork for.

SOURCING PROPS

A lot of times, I've had people tell me that they're not able to style a frame beautifully because they don't have too many props. Firstly, you can never have too many props. Secondly, you don't need a treasure trove of props to style a picture. You'll be surprised to see how much a basic glass bottle, a bunch of flowers from the garden, a crumpled newspaper or a burlap can add to a frame. Most of the large department stores like HomeCentre have a great collection of cheap but pretty plates. They also stock things like jars, bottles and chopping boards. For those living in Delhi, Khurja is a great place to source ceramics from. Stores like Nicobar also have a great collection of tableware. Their marble cake stand and cheese boards make for great props. In Mumbai, Clove – The Store is my favourite because you find so many brands under the same roof. During my visits to Mumbai, I've also picked a few interesting things from Mitti in Andheri West.

As someone who calls himself a food stylist, I don't have a massive collection myself. I often reuse and recycle.

I have built my collection over time by picking a few things from the stores if I spot anything interesting, sitting down to hunt for pretty tableware online and getting backpacks full of ceramics from my travels abroad. I've also made trips to small shops in Old Delhi to pick up rustic metallic props. I also go to scrap shops because I always find something interesting there. Sourcing props is a lot of fun and you don't always need to spend a lot of money on getting something for your pictures. I remember picking up a knife I love from a small street shop in Bangalore that I just happened to cross. In Indonesia, I convinced a grain seller to barter an old can he was using to measure grains by getting him a brand new one. You just need to keep your eyes open.

FROSTING

Frosting a cake intimidates a lot of people. Here are six important tips to make your frosting work look professional, and worth the time and effort.

ALWAYS PUT STRIPS OF BUTTER PAPER BENEATH THE EDGES OF THE CAKE

Before you start with anything else, it is important that you prepare your workstation for all the mess that could potentially take place. I hate it when I pause in the middle of the work to see things spilling or getting messy. This is why I always put strips of butter paper or wax paper beneath the edges of the cakes to avoid the frosting from spilling onto the surface below. You can easily take them off later when you are done.

ENSURE FLAT TOPS BEFORE FILLING OR FROSTING

If you plan to decorate your cake with toppings or icing, it always makes more sense to have a levelled top. It makes it easier to stack your requirements and give a more professional look to your ensemble. Be very sure that the top is even so that the frosting looks smooth. You can always upturn the bottom to the top to get the levelled look.

CRUMB COATING IS A MUST

It never fails to surprise me how a lot of people think it is okay to go ahead with just one layer of frosting on your cake. Don't let it fool you; your cake will always have crumbs falling out of it. Which is why you should crumb-coat cakes with frosting. The first layer of frosting is meant to hold your cake together and give it a base for the final, unblemished layer of frosting.

COOLING PERIOD AFTER CRUMB COATING IS ESSENTIAL

Patience is key. Once you have crumb-coated your cake, allow it to cool for some time so that the layer becomes considerably firm and hard. The point of crumb-coating is to provide an even base for your final layer of frosting. Unless the base is stiff enough to hold the outer layer, your cake could turn out to look ragged.

START FROM THE CENTRE TO THE EDGES, ALWAYS

An important tip while frosting or filling is to always drop a scoop in the centre and work your way out, rather than spreading alongside the edges first. Take your offset spatula and flatten the frosting while gradually pushing it towards the edges. The excess on the sides could be pushed downwards to coat the sides of your cake and lock in the crumbs that are likely to appear. Make sure you run your spatula around the sides to make it as even as possible.

Also, remember to not entirely reach the ends when you are filling in a layered cake. This is because too much frosting and filling till the edges could make the frosting spill when you stack another layer on top.

DIP THE OFFSET SPATULA IN A JAR OF WARM WATER

One helpful tip that I employ is to dip in my spatula in a jar of warm water for a few minutes and then wipe and use it to make the frosting look neat and even. The warmed-up spatula will minimally melt the upper layer of frosting to smoothen the surface, making it look refined.

TOOLS

1. Paper towels: Dealing with food gets messy and that is where these come in handy.

2. Tweezers: While styling, you may want to move tiny things around and using a pair of tweezers ensures that you move only what is needed.

3. Brushes: I use these to clean the surface I'm shooting on or for dusting away crumbs. They also come in handy when I've to freshen up the dessert I'm shooting.

4. Knives and cutting boards: You'll need knives and boards for slicing the dessert or fruits that you may use in your image.

5. Coins: A lot of times, the objects close to the edges of your frame look tilted, giving your image a slightly deformed look. Use coins to straighten these objects.

6. Water-spray bottles: These are useful if you're shooting fresh ingredients. A few water droplets on freshly cut fruits add freshness. To show condensation on cold objects, rub Vaseline on the surface before spraying water, the droplets will stay longer.

7. Small offset spatula: The offset spatula helps fix the frosting and get the swirls.

8. Small sieve: You'll need this for dusting icing sugar on desserts.

9. Kitchen blowtorch: This will help you beautifully toast that meringue. Also, it's so much fun to use!

10. Gloves: For handling glass objects, always wear gloves or use tissue paper to avoid leaving fingerprints.

STEP 1: I started by keeping the cake stand bang in the centre of the frame but it was looking too crowded and boring.

STEP 2: I tried pushing the cake stand to the side and also played around with the backgrounds. The frame was still looking very flat – it lacked height and depth.

STEP 3: I pushed the cake stand to the back and also added two plates in the frame. It also helped me introduce different heights.

STEP 4: I completed the frame by adding ingredients and elements that complement the apple muffins – oats, peanut butter, coffee and cinnamon sticks

ADD HUMAN ELEMENT
ADD
INGREDIENTS

HANDMADE FLAGS
USING SKEWER
AND BURLAP

ADD DETAILS–
FRESHLY GRATED
LEMON ZEST

STYLE WITH SHIVESH 02

STEP 1: I started by placing the cake on a distressed white table against a plain white background.

STEP 2: Not too sure of my choice, I decided to experiment with a darker theme. I changed the set-up to incorporate dark wood and added citrus to add vibrancy.

STEP 3: I added a knife to make the dessert look more accessible. The lemon in the front was a distraction, so I cut it into half.

STEP 4: The lemon curd on the top layer was making the cake untidy. So, I cleaned that up and decided to go ahead with only whipped cream on top, giving it a cleaner look.

STEP 1: I chose a summery yet rustic theme for this image and started by first placing the dessert. Added some oranges, dried orange slices and the gooseberry compote jar.

STEP 2: I got rid of the dried oranges as they were not complementing the freshness of the photo. The white bowl in the front adds more depth to the photo and the tall jar at the back adds height.

STEP 3: I cut into the cake to reveal its texture. This is particularly interesting for a dessert like the chiffon cake here because it has a beautiful, airy texture.

STEP 4: Once I got a good shot of the cake, I took a flat lay of the slices and gooseberry compote. The out-of-focus tree coming in from one of the corners of the frame makes it interesting.

FOR FRESHNESS AND DEPTH

CUTLERY TO MAKE THE CAKE LOOK ACCESSIBLE

PHOTOGRAPHY

Bring out your phones and cameras, your dessert is ready for its photoshoot.

PHOTOGRAPHY

I shoot all my pictures on my Canon 700D with a 50-mm lens. I started by taking pictures on my iPad but made a switch to the DSLR once I started shooting for brands. I also used a point-and-shoot camera very briefly but wasn't happy with the images. Using a DSLR allows me to achieve a lot of depth in my picture.

However, I always look at equipment as an enabler rather than a disabler. It should aid you and not limit you or stop you from producing images. If you can, invest in a good camera but if you cannot, it doesn't mean you can't shoot! Pick up whatever you have – it could just be a smartphone with a camera. There is no end to how much you can invest in equipment. We live in an age where technology is limitless and there'll be a new camera in the market every day. Don't make not having an expensive camera an excuse and don't let that keep you away from clicking pictures. If you're planning to invest in a camera, make sure you do your research. Ask around to see what others are using. If possible, borrow their camera for a day and play around with it. Getting hands-on experience with the device will help you make the best decision.

I also try and use a tripod as often as I can. I found using a tripod very restricting initially but I do realize that it helps me capture sharp images. No matter how sturdy your grip is, you may end up moving a little when you click and that results in a blurry picture. That blur may or may not be visible on a camera screen but it will be visible when you view it on a bigger screen.

Now, you may wonder how much time you should spend on shooting one picture? Ideally, don't set a time limit for yourself. Simply have fun with photography and take your own sweet time in getting the shot that makes you happy. Shooting under pressure is not a great idea and that should happen only when you're shooting icecreams! However, it so happens sometimes that you're just not able to get the right shot. This could be because of the styling or because of the photography or because you're just not feeling it. What I've felt in these cases is that the one-hour rule works for me. If shooting for one hour doesn't get me the desired results, I just take a break and get on to something else. Coming back to that same dessert with a fresh mind helps me get a better shot.

THREE PILLARS OF PHOTOGRAPHY

ISO

ISO is the level of sensitivity of your camera to light. A lower ISO means a lower sensitivity to light and higher ISO means higher sensitivity to light. It is usually displayed in a range of 100-6400.
It is ideal to always keep the ISO as low as you can because it gives you a finer quality of picture. Increasing the ISO too much can make your image grainy.

A lower ISO is great to take moody images. I also stick to a lower ISO like 100 or 200 when there is too much light. A higher ISO when there is too much light results in overexposed pictures.

A higher ISO allows you to take pictures in low light without having to use an external flash. You can increase it when there is not enough light but that comes with some noise in the photograph.

APERTURE

The aperture is the size of the opening in the lens and is measured using 'f-stops' like (f/2.8), (f/16). There is an inverse relation between the aperture and the f-stops.
A larger aperture is indicated by a small f-number and a small aperture is indicated by a large f-number.

The size of the aperture helps to control the amount of light entering the camera. It also helps to control the depth of field or the area of the image that is in focus.

A smaller f-number will help you achieve a shallow depth of field where only a small part of the picture will be in focus and the background will be blurred.

A larger f-number creates a larger depth of field where the entire image will be equally in focus. Also, a smaller f-number allows more light while a larger f-number allows less light to pass through the lens.

SHUTTER SPEED

It is the time that your camera's shutter remains open while taking a picture. A higher shutter speed (for example, 1/1000 seconds) helps you freeze the motion of moving objects while a slower shutter speed (for example, 1/60 seconds) will blur the motion.

UNDERSTAND LIGHT

I believe light is the factor that differentiates a good image from a great image. I always shoot in natural light. Using the light from tube lights, bulbs or an external flash ruins the colour and texture of the food in the photograph. Using professional lights is a different ball game altogether, but if you don't have that kind of expertise, strictly stick to shooting in natural light only. I normally bake at night and shoot in the morning before anyone gets the chance to attack the dessert.

Whenever you're shooting, make sure the light is not too harsh. If it is, it will cast heavy shadows on the picture. Professional photographers recommend shooting in the golden hour, which is the period shortly after sunrise or before sunset when the light is soft and perfect for photography. Since I sometimes shoot three to four desserts in a day, that short window doesn't always work for me. I shoot throughout the day but make sure I have enough natural light where I'm shooting; also that it is not too harsh. To avoid harsh light, you can get a diffuser or simply use some sheer curtain or a thin sheet on the light source.

WHERE SHOULD THE LIGHT SOURCE BE?

When I am shooting I usually set-up in a way that the light falls on my food either from the side or from the back. Doing so ensures that you get some shadows in the picture. I usually shoot next to a door or window so that I get an ample amount of side light. In case the other side (the one away from the light source) feels too dark, I simply fix a sheet of aluminium foil facing the light source. The foil works as a reflector and bounces back the light, making sure the other side gets enough light.You can also use a thermocol sheet as a reflector. If light is falling equally on your food from all sides, the picture will end up looking flat and boring. Avoid placing yourself between the source of light and the food. It'll cast your shadow on the set-up, making the food look dull.

You should try experimenting with backlight. Set up in a way that the source of light is behind the food. It creates some drama in the picture and usually the results with backlighting are very interesting because of the way the shadows fall.

USEFUL TIPS

SHOOT IN RAW

I used to away from shooting in RAW (a RAW image file contains minimally processed data). Don't ask me why, I just assumed that shooting in RAW would be more difficult. As a matter of fact, it isn't. It has nothing to do with your photography process but makes your editing much simpler and the quality much better. When an image is shot in JPEG, the image information is compressed and a lot of it is lost. When you shoot in RAW, you're able to record a lot more information about the images. It not only helps you produce the highest quality images but also have greater control and flexibility when you're post-processing them.

MOVE AWAY FROM AUTO

As I said, I'm not a very technical person and I'm still discovering the wonders a camera can do. My photography changed completely once I decided to not be intimidated by all those buttons. I was shooting on auto mode for the longest time and avoided understanding technical terms like ISO, aperture and shutter speed. But then I decided to switch from auto to shooting in manual and realized I was missing out on so much. The fact that you can change and tweak every single element – the amount of light that comes in, the speed of your shutter and the focal length – changed photography for me. I'm still learning new things every day. Don't be afraid to make the switch from auto. It will take you some time (or a lot of time if you're a dummy like me) but it'll be worth the confusion and you will see the results in your final images.

ACTION SHOTS

I love shots that show some action; it makes the frame fun and more exciting. Capturing the pouring of maple syrup on pancakes or dusting of sugar on tea cakes looks wonderful but is slightly tricky. It is all about the timing and technique. You need to work fast to make sure you capture the movement perfectly on camera.

Here are some tips to get the hang of action shots:

1. On the right are two images – one is blurred and the other a near-perfect capture. In the blurred image, my shutter speed was 1/40 seconds while in the other it was 1/1000 seconds. The trick to getting the shot right is to shoot at a high shutter speed. The high shutter speed helps you freeze the movement, resulting in a crystal-clear capture of each single grain or droplet.

2. To make sure you don't miss the perfect moment, change your camera settings to 'continuous shooting' from 'single shot'. I usually set the number of shots to 10 shots in 10 seconds. That way you're able to capture the action 10 times and this ensures you're able to freeze every little movement in the frame.

3. You could get someone to help you with the movement while you're in charge of the camera. But sometimes, when no one is available, I drizzle the sugar and pour the sauce on my own. Since the camera is fixed on the tripod, I'm able to play both roles. I set the camera on a 10-second timer, choose the continuous shooting mode and capture an action shot single-handedly.

4. Fix the camera to a tripod. When you're clicking action shots, a tripod becomes essential. Since there is already some movement in the frame, you don't want any movement in your camera. Having a tripod makes it easier to avoid the blur and capture the movement right in time. Anyway not having to hold the camera with both your hands helps you work quicker.

5. Usually, action shots look better against a contrasting background. It makes the picture more vivid. Capturing drizzling sugar or steam against a dark background will produce much better results than shooting them against a white one.

EXPERIMENT WITH DEPTH OF FIELD

Experimenting with depth of field helps you focus on a single area. This creates an interesting depth in the picture and guides the viewer's eyes to what you want them to see. This technique is particularly helpful when you don't have anything exciting in the background.

When everything in a picture is equally in focus, it ends up looking slightly flat. The solution is to switch to aperture priority mode and manually tweak the aperture to determine the area that will be in focus. A shallow depth of field focuses on a smaller area. So, if you want only a smaller part of the image to be in focus, you need to go for a lower f-stop. I usually go for a shallow depth of field when I'm taking a front-angle shot. For flat lays or top-angle pictures, I usually go for a deeper depth of field and have everything in focus.

PHONE PHOTOGRAPHY

These days all of us own good phones with great cameras. I use my phone to shoot all my food pictures when I'm travelling or when I'm eating out. I also shoot on the phone sometimes for my Instagram or blog. It is easier to shoot, edit and post from your phone. I use an iPhone 8+ or an iPhone X for food photography.

Keep the following factors in mind when shooting with a smartphone camera:

BE STURDY

It is very important to have a firm grip on your phone while shooting. Since you can't fix your phone on a tripod (there are tripods for phones, though!), a sturdy grip becomes crucial to ensure that your pictures are sharp and crisp. Use both your hands to hold the phone in place and ensure there is no shake. If you're shooting on an iPhone, you could also use the volume buttons, which reduces the chances of shaking.

FOCUS

One aspect of getting a clear and sharp picture is to focus it right. Decide which part of the image you want to focus on. Simply tap on that area on the screen of your smartphone and allow the camera to focus before you click. Make sure you do this every time you take a picture.

TRY TAKING A TOP-ANGLE SHOT

The top angle works best for me when shooting on a phone. A flat lay of the table with everyone's food makes for a great shot. Make sure you hold your phone precisely parallel to the surface you're shooting on, otherwise you'll get a deformed image. Sometimes it becomes difficult to take a top-angle shot while trying to press the click button. In such cases, putting a timer on the phone helps.

ADJUST THE LIGHT

Most phones allow you to adjust the light in the frame. Simply tap the frame and pull it down to decrease the light and push it upwards for more light. Avoid using the flash on the phone while shooting food. If you're trying to take a picture of your food in a restaurant, try grabbing a table close to a window. If it is too dark, use the flash light from a friend's phone to light the frame. Doing this is a better option than using the flash on your own phone because you can adjust the distance and direction of the other person's flashlight. Another hack is to place a sheer napkin in front of the flashlight in case it is too harsh.

DO NOT ZOOM IN

When you're shooting on the phone, it helps to hold the phone closer to the food. This helps me achieve a macro shot, something like a 50-mm lens on a DSLR would. Remember to not use the digital zoom. Most phones allow you to zoom in by using your fingers but unlike the optical zoom on a DSLR, this is a digital zoom. Zooming in adversely effects the quality of the picture. To take a zoomed-in shot, simply move closer to the food and shoot. I prefer cropping out the unnecessary parts when I'm post-processing the image.

CLEAN YOUR LENS

Since your smartphone is in your pocket or hands the entire day, the camera lens gets dirty. Phone cameras are exposed to dust, grease and fingerprints. If the camera lens is dirty, you will end up having smudges and spots on your pictures. Most of us don't realize when this happens, so as a rule, make sure you clean your lens every time you shoot on your phone. A clean camera lens is very important to give you a clear and sharp image.

EXPERIMENT WITH DIFFERENT FEATURES

A lot of smartphones have different features that will help you take better pictures of your food. Play around and experiment with different features and modes. I love using the portrait mode on my iPhone X. It gives the picture the much-needed depth of field by keeping my dessert in focus and blurring the background. I avoid using the portrait mode when the distinction between the subject and background is not very clear or if I'm shooting desserts in glasses. The HDR feature on most phones allows you to achieve a sharper image. Whenever I'm trying to capture an action shot on my phone, I use the burst mode.

EDIT RIGHT

I edit my phone pictures on VSCO Cam and Snapseed. VSCO has some great filters that work beautifully on food pictures. F2 is my favourite. I avoid using the filters on Instagram as they do not work very well on food pictures. Instagram is otherwise great for basic editing like tweaking the brightness, contrast and sharpness. Increasing the 'structure' on Instagram brings the photo alive. Snapseed allows me to do selective retouching on my images. If you want to edit the RAW camera images, LightRoom is a great option. I learnt working on light room by playing around with the features. I particularly like 'vibrance' that helps me improve the colours of my photo and 'vignette' that darkens and improves my moody shots.

ACKNOWLEDGEMENTS

It has always been a dream to have a book of my own and I'm so grateful to finally see it coming to life. This has been the most exciting and challenging journey and I have a long list of people to thank for making it all the more special.

My mummy, for being my rock. Thank you for pushing me to work harder and for telling me to always believe in myself. I know you will be the happiest to see this book come to life and I can't wait for you to hold a copy in your hands. Truly, I couldn't have done this without you. *Bake with Shivesh* is yours as much as mine.

Papa, thank you for making sure I got everything I needed to work on this book. You've always supported my decisions and have encouraged me to follow my dreams. Thank you for being the coolest parent ever!

My grandparents and my twin, Shubhra, for always being by my side.

My cousin Malika and my friends Shreya, Gunjan, Sahiba, Radhika, Rukmini, Lyimee, Himansh, Shruti, Varun, Ankrish, Khadija and Trisha, for being my support system. I'm so grateful to have each one of you in my life. Thank you for always being there when I need you – you're the best friends and the most efficient tasters ever!

Navrup, for jumping in when I most needed help. Thank you for testing and retesting the recipes with me. You made working on this book so much easier.

My editor Shreya Punj, for believing that I could write a book. I can't thank you enough for giving me this opportunity and for making my dream of writing a book come true. Thank you for being my mentor and, most importantly, a friend who told me I could do this.

The entire team at HarperCollins for your knowledge and for being so patient. I could not have asked for a better team to work with. Bonita, Keku, Isha, Divya – thank you for all the support.

Most importantly, the wonderful people on my Instagram and readers of my blog- this couldn't have been possible without your unconditional love and support over the years. You make me believe in myself and give me the confidence to follow my dreams – I can't thank you guys enough for that.

INDEX

INDEX